STAR CHILDREN

STAR CHILDREN

Understanding children who set us
special tasks and challenges

Georg Kühlewind

TEMPLE LODGE

Translated from German by Pauline Wehrle

Temple Lodge Publishing
Hillside House, The Square
Forest Row, RH18 5ES

www.templelodge.com

First published in English by Temple Lodge 2004
Reprinted 2005

Originally published in German under the title *Sternkinder, Kinder, die uns besondere Aufgaben stellen* by Verlag Freies Geistesleben, Stuttgart, in 2001

© Verlag Freies Geistesleben & Urachhaus GmbH, Stuttgart, 2001

A catalogue record for this book is available from the British Library

ISBN 1 902636 49 X

Cover by Andrew Morgan
Typeset by DP Photosetting, Aylesbury, Bucks.
Printed and bound in Cromwell Press Limited, Trowbridge, Wilts.

Contents

Translator's Foreword

I found this book really exciting. Georg Kühlewind tells us that for about the past 20 years a new generation of children has been coming to earth in growing numbers, a happening which he calls the most important of our age. And in order to give us the necessary background with which to follow what he has to say about these star children he takes us consciously, scientifically, into the realm from which we all enter the world, as babies 'trailing clouds of glory...' We all possess the tools he describes for taking this path: our thoughts, our heart forces and our willpower. And by using these with our full attention, and focusing our attentiveness and eliminating everything else, we can enter the realm which is the realm of the spirit where laws differing from those on earth prevail. For the sake of acquiring individual freedom we need to live for a while in the earthly world which has become a world of duality, of realities of an outer and an inner kind, of communication that requires speech and language, writing and signs. The world of the spirit, however, is a world of unity, of direct communication requiring no signs, where the meaning of things and the creative process are at home. This difference between the two worlds is why a mere observation of small children's behaviour will not supply us with an understanding of them, steeped as we are in our sense of self, and the resulting self-interest. So Georg Kühlewind helps us along the path to an inner understanding by giving us, at the close of each short chapter, themes for contemplation and for meditation which are most helpful. I strongly recommend spending a few minutes working at them. They encourage a leap into the other dimension.

Those who read this book with expectations of being given all the info required to master the subject of star children may be left with a sense of disappointment that the author devotes so much space to describing small children in general and so little to star children as such. In his defence I would like to underline that he himself says that this book is a first attempt to write about star children, and research will and must continue. As for myself, I feel that we are being helped so much to open our inner eyes to a wider and wider view of the spirit, of the religious sense, of what a sense of respect and awe means, of what we are and can become in our own being, etc., etc. Yet all this and more — in fact the willpower to make these values real in our human world — will be essential if we are to give these children who are joining us in increasing numbers the kind of welcome necessary for them to have a chance to do what they come to do.

P.W.

Setting the mood

How this book came about

If we have children of our own we are amazed every day at their progress, at the rapid strides in their 'development'. The quotation marks are intended to express the fact that development is meant in a double sense, indicating both the transforming of consciousness into that of an adult and, running parallel with this, the successive loss of the natural inspirations which are an innate capacity of early childhood. The sensitive measuring stick of this process is the young child's speech, and not by a long way only its verbal language, but everything belonging to its intentional expressions. This extends, for example, from eye contact and smiling to consciously refraining from crying.

The variety of wonders to do with acquiring speech[1] and, related to this, the significance of egoity[2] – i.e. of the ego body which is coming into being, and with whose help the human being begins to feel himself as a subject able to confront the world – it is these wonders that moved me to do research, and they still do to this day.[3] The theme of the small child here touches on that of the oldest of traditions: paradise and the Fall – direct, signless communication and audible speech.

For many years human attentiveness has been my principal theme. A small child's attentiveness soon became my point of departure for understanding both the processes an adult experiences as well as existence before birth. What do we mean by 'language' in the pre-birth realm, what is our state of being[4] in the so-called Beyond, and how does the 'state of being' turn into the ability to understand or to express ourselves on earth?

The chief impulse for my research on the life of consciousness of a small child, prepared by way of the studies I have mentioned, was my recent insight which also led to the founding of the Logos Foundation;[5] namely the following: In the pre-birth realm we live entirely among ego beings whose existence and being are identical with their expression (language) in the same way as we ourselves all exist in a 'speaking' condition in a world realm consisting altogether only of meaning and significance. Then we are born on earth where the only ego beings are human beings—and to what extent have we already become human? That is the actual trauma at our birth, and to this day I still do not know how we stand it or survive it.

There is something else as well. To small children in general, to those who are autistic at an early age, to many dyslexics, and star children right up until adulthood or beyond, we are as it were transparent. They 'see'—feel— our weak spots, even those we are not aware of ourselves. They sense when we are not being entirely honest, or when we are pretending. And for them that is a second trauma.

Why is it so difficult to understand small children?

We have such little understanding of the consciousness or the spirit/soul of a small child because our consciousness has changed so much since our early childhood. Our intelligence and that of the small child have about the same kind of relationship to one another as a pile of small change has to a cheque which contains the sum total all in one amount—there is hardly any similarity. Where the difference lies and how it comes about will be developed in the course of this book. The fundamental question is how the adult can find out about small children's consciousness. For the simplest theories fail in practice, meaning that they do not lead to the desired results. It is no good knowing theoretically how to skate — for without personal experience on the ice you will not be able to take one single step.

Star children

While working on this book the following happened to me: As I checked in at the airport in Hamburg a young couple was in front of me, and the mother had a three-to-four month old baby in her arms. All of a sudden the baby turned round and looked at me. He looked me straight in the eye, and I was deeply shaken; for that was not the look of a baby but of a very self-aware adult, a wise one, and he appeared to see right through me. I had encountered a penetrating look of that sort before in the case of people with acute autism.

This experience remained on my mind, and I remembered a number of other such intense experiences of eye contact with children, also older ones. Then it occurred to me how often teachers both in school and in kindergartens had complained that they were increasingly encountering children who were difficult but also very gifted. At the same time as this the Californian book on the so-called 'indigo children' fell into my hands, and then too a book by Henning Köhler. And it came home to me that for about the last twenty years (with a few forerunners) a new generation of children has been coming to earth in growing numbers, and that this is the most important happening of our age. Thus my attention swung from a study of the nature of small children in general, to focus more and more on these new children—whom I have called 'star children'—and you will see why. It seemed to me that to write about them would be the most important thing to do, because a great many teachers, psychologists and psychiatrists (anthroposophical ones included) not only do not notice what the problem is when they are faced with 'difficult' children but sometimes do not even want to notice. In the meantime more than seventy 'technical terms' had been coined to describe them. Troublesome children are often enough diagnosed as being brain-damaged and given medication to suppress the symptoms, but this at the same time destroys the possibilities and impulses these children bring with them. Not every difficult child is a star child, of course, but the majority of them certainly are.

Therefore the focal point of my work while writing this book has shifted in the direction of star children—and I have to admit that this is a first attempt. Research will and must continue. I am indebted to Henning Köhler for the corroberation the opinions I have expressed have received from his enormous experience with problem children.

So as to be able to present the spirit/soul nature of star children in a comprehensible manner I must start by dealing with the spiritual nature of small children in general.

Method of research

Researching the consciousness of a small child cannot consist in merely observing its behaviour, for observation always takes place by way of adult consciousness which has been trained to make use of the kind of conceptual images at its disposal. These concepts, however, differ both in quality and quantity from the 'conceptual images' of small children, which determine their behaviour to the same extent as adults' concepts determine their observation. If adults cannot experience the soul constitution of the small child — at least its main features — they cannot do otherwise than interpret its behaviour (the object of their observation) wrongly, in fact they already 'see' it wrongly, as what is seen is largely determined and interpreted by the seer.

The path and the method of spiritual investigation is simple but demanding. It consists of an infinitely intensified concentration, first of the thinking/visualizing attentiveness, then of the feeling attentiveness and finally of the attentiveness of the will, where thinking, feeling and will interpenetrate one another from the start, and gradually pass over into one another in the order described.

This concentration raises us stepwise into the present, which we otherwise never really experience because presence of mind — even that of understanding — is as short as a flash of lightning. Experiencing the lightning through its lengthening, we are aware of how our attentiveness streams into the theme of the focus of attention — a mental image or a thought — in order to bring it forth and hold it. We find that the theme consists of our attentiveness, that is, solely of our own self. For it is our spiritual being that is the attentiveness.[6] We experience our identity with the theme. This is the experience of identity stripped of all signs and words, a pure *object* that is us — that we *are* in so far as we are in perpetual becoming. We are the meaning of the theme, or rather we shall become it — not a sign of the theme or rather of its manifestation — and that sets off the experience of a consecutive string of transformations. On the one hand we experience our wakeful spiritual self as an 'I am' experience, without this 'I am' needing an object through which it can experience itself as another — which is particularly the case with the everyday ego, which does experience itself through the other. Secondly the theme changes into a continuous becoming. In the course of further practice by strengthening the flow of attentiveness both kinds of experience change continually. The 'I am' changes from being a concept-free intuitive thinking into the colour of perceptive feeling, then continually into perceptive willing; and parallel with this the theme turns into feeling, into a 'felt idea' and later to a will form. A formative will lives in everything that has form.

These qualitative changes in experience run through the various phases of the small child's experience of the world, but now in a self-conscious form. By means of concentration and meditation we can discover how the small child experiences the world, if we cancel out the losing of our attitude of devotion which we lost in the course of growing up.[7]

Practical indications for the reader

The full content of this book will only come about through the active participation of the reader in doing his/her own contemplating and meditating. Exercises for 'contemplation' and 'meditation' are presented within the text. The former are thoughts which one deepens through further thought, the latter are sentences for meditation which one can and should think about before one meditates them.

Meditation consists in concentrating one's forces on the sentence, that is, on its wordless meaning above language, on the force of the sentence which one can also call one's 'sun', for it must be there 'earlier' than its formulation, the words and the grammatical idiom. Our consciousness finds these by means of the sun. In concentrating without words and language on the meaning of the sentence this meaning can become transparent and a further level of meaning can light up. Meanwhile this concentrated, purposeful attentiveness is transformed into a momentarily empty and receptive one. This makes possible the appearance of the next level of meaning. In this sense the meditation can be an exercise for acquiring a more intuitive consciousness, or it can be used for research.

I
A PHENOMENOLOGICAL STUDY OF THE NATURE OF THE SMALL CHILD

1.
What do the words 'spiritual' and 'spiritual beings' mean?

When we are born a spiritual being unites with an inherited body — as many people say, but just as many say and even more people think that there is no such thing as a spiritual being. It is therefore relevant to investigate and describe the term 'spiritual' in greater detail.

The best way is to look at language. Every language — including gestures, the arts, the expression in the eyes, and suchlike — consists of sense-perceptible signs and non-sense-perceptible meanings. Signs have a material mediator (air, waves, paper, ink, etc.) whereas the meanings are free of material substance; we can search in vain for any kind of material they might be made of. By 'meaning' we understand not only what can be conveyed by verbal language but also what appeals only to feeling, like for instance music or other such arts, or to the perceptive will, like for example a religious ritual. The latter meanings cannot be translated into a verbal language — otherwise music etc. would be replaceable, i.e. superfluous.

When we hear or read a foreign language which we do not understand we only take in the signs. Fairytales obviously speak to people's feelings, otherwise it would be incomprehensible why adults, too, can become totally absorbed by them.

If meaning is free of material substance and yet an indubitable reality which is the origin of the signs — for a sign cannot exist without a meaning, yet at the time of coming into being the meaning has not yet acquired a sign — then this reality can be called 'spiritual'; it is both free of substance *and* understandable, meaningful. It follows directly from this that the source of meanings can also not be material, and also just as little can the person who comprehends meaning be material. On the other hand signs and meaning are not customarily joined together mechanically[8] — a sign can of course have very different meanings all according to the context and circumstances — so understanding and a person who understands are components of the phenomenon 'sign-meaning'. It follows then that neither understanding nor the person who understands can be material. Understanding is a spiritual phenomenon and a person who understands is a spiritual being.[9] If a person who can read and another person who cannot read look at the same text, or if a chess-player or someone who does not know how to play it look at a configuration on the chess-board, the difference in what they see is not that the first people see a *material connection (or a connection of forces)* between the letters or words or between the chess figures which is hidden from the others. If you hear someone saying: 'That is a good story!' the meaning depends on the circumstances described, for the wording by itself does not determine anything.

Themes for contemplation:

1. A monkey understands the words for numbers up to seven. If you say 'six' to it, it will give six knocks. Is it a spiritual being? What would it have to be capable of doing for us to recognize it as a spiritual being?
2. Can you say something, see something, imagine something that has no meaning? Is there such a thing as something that has no meaning?
3. What realities do we know that are free of material substance?
4. Where signs are concerned, their configuration, their

form, is what is characteristic of them, is their nature a sign, and not or only seldom the material they are made of. What sort of things can be signs?

Themes for meditation:
1. Only meanings can be understood.
2. The difference between effect and sign is in the understanding.

2.
Is a baby a spiritual being?

Understanding cannot be taught, since all teaching pre-supposes the capacity to understand. If the potential for understanding is not there then understanding cannot unfold. A baby comes into the world tuned in for under-standing or attuned to meaning. This can be seen in that right from the beginning it understands signs, or to be more exact, understands the meanings of signs, and it does so in fact long before it can express meanings verbally or in any other way. The first sign is eye contact, the 'meaning' of which is too great to be expressed in words; and so is the next sign in life, that of responding to a smile with an answering smile. All the other non-inherited capacities which appear later, such as standing upright, walking on two feet,[10] speaking or thinking, touch in any case on the field of tension between sign and meaning, that is, they presuppose understanding.

If we look closely at these abilities we can, from the fact of their appearance, draw two conclusions. The first is that the child brings them with it, and this points to an existence before birth: as a spiritual being it already existed before birth but was not yet bound to a body. With the second conclusion we take into consideration that this spiritual being enters a world which is constructed on the pattern of language, and which therefore contains both material substance and meaning. In a spiritual world, a world of spiritual beings who create and understand meanings, there exist no signs; if only for the reason that material substance does not exist there—this is a realm of silent language and of direct and immediate understanding.[11]

Right from birth, however, the spiritual being of the child is attuned to the earthly world, that is, to a world that contains material substance and, in consequence, signs. The baby encounters signs and is no stranger to them, for it 'looks' for their meaning and sense. It brings something like an implicit, non-specific 'knowledge' of the earthly world with it. This is evident not only in the various spheres in which its capacities lie, such as music, mathematics, etc.[12] but also in the fact that the child usually finds its way effortlessly into the basic nature of the earthly world—namely the fact that it consists of signs and meanings alongside one another. The way it familiarizes itself with the world is obviously recognition and does not point to an arrival in a totally alien world. A spiritual being is a being that can understand meanings; that expects there to be meanings behind the signs, and looks for an understanding of them.

Have you ever experienced a baby smiling at you?

Themes for contemplation:
5. How does the child know that sense perceptible signs, like smiling, have meaning?
6. Every form of caring for the child presupposes love, otherwise the child will feel it to be a pretence, which in fact it is. Love for the child is either there or it is not. What can we do in the latter case?
7. The child can imitate signs like sounds and words without understanding their meaning. What does this show?

Theme for meditation:
3. What is 'understanding'?

3.
The Good in a child

In older cultures in the East, in Zen as well as the European tradition of Plato, Aristotle and Thomas Aquinas, Good was the highest real force principle according to which the world was constructed and the human being was created.[13] The world of signs, usually called 'world', was gradually handed over to human beings particularly by way of Christianity. Although He is almighty — 'with God all things are possible' — the Godhead interferes neither in the fate of the world nor of human beings, if humanity or individual human beings do not call for help. Obviously if the Godhead does give help He gives it through human agency. But the natural course of the world, in so far as it can work in human beings as an implicit knowledge of the Good, contains the possibility of an orientation towards the Good. Every conception of 'karma' or destiny presupposes that the world and the human being is so orientated, otherwise 'creating a balance' would have no meaning.

Even if we consider it from a different aspect it is not difficult to see that in the dualistically-formed system of thought and language the positive pole is primary. Without an experience of light, of the good, beautiful, true and meaningful, we would not know their opposites or perceive the opposite qualities. Taking light as an example: darkness becomes visible to us because we have the gift of seeing the light and because it is possible to know of light. If we lived only in darkness we would neither be aware of darkness nor have any conception of light. In this sense a baby, too, comes into the world as a spiritual being orientated towards the Good. This comes to expression in a baby's openness and capacity for devotion, or in other words its 'love'.[14] At least until the appearance of egoity (see chapter 11) an orientation towards the Good can be observed in a baby. Though of course in a civilization governed by the principle of egoity (which is even considered a sound thing) one has to have sharp eyes to see it. If one has, then one can confirm that every human being does not only come into the world 'lighted by the true light' (John 1,9) but with the full intention of bringing the maximum Good to the world and their fellow human beings. Whilst growing up this intention is often covered over or deflected by life and education or even turned into its opposite. It is plain to see, however, that small children grasp the word Good in its many applications without needing any explanations at all—which, as adults, we would not be capable of giving, anyway, nor could children understand them.

Theme for contemplation:
8. Un-good, un-beautiful, un-true—un-bad, un-ugly, un-wrong... Continue the sequence. How can we perceive the basic disposition of a small child (under two)?

Theme for meditation:
4. Can we explain or define the Good? If not, where does the concept come from?

4.
Non-inherited factors

We have mentioned that the specifically human capacities of eye contact, smiling, standing upright, walking and speaking followed by thinking, are not inherited. They all only unfold in a normal human environment. The potential for them must already be present in the child, and this leads to the question as to *how* and in what way they are present potentially. It is worthy of note that the capacities mentioned are all soul activities or — in the case of speaking and thinking — soul/spiritual activities which come to manifestation through the body. Standing upright and walking on two feet are, from the biological point of view, superfluous, even 'impractical' ways of behaving. They are not biologically inherited, otherwise they would either appear infallibly in every case, just as the teeth do, or be called forth by biological/physical circumstances (just as a seed sprouts in warmth and dampness).

These capacities do, of course, have biological prerequisites, like nourishment, bodily care, etc. But these are not sufficient to make them appear. What is needed is the soul/spiritual attention of an environment of adult human beings, their attentiveness. Without this, these capacities will not develop. Devoted attention can overcome the greatest bodily hindrances, such as simultaneous blindness and deafness — Helen Keller is an impressive example of this — whilst a lack of human attention can sometimes lead to lifelong handicap even if all the bodily prerequisites are present. These phenomena of the developing faculties could of course be explained by imitation, if the very capacity to imitate specific human abilities did not happen to be itself in question: namely the existence of an initial given possibility which animals do not have.

From the foregoing descriptions it emerges that what the child brings with it, the 'germinal beginnings' of the above-mentioned capacities, are to be sought not among the inherited traits but in the baby's spiritual being, and that the sole aim of education is to unite this spiritual being and its capacities with the inherited body, so that the 'germinal abilities' can be made manifest by the body as observable, operative capacities, and the body can be used as an instrument of signs for the varying meanings of the inner life or the spiritual being. In other words: that the spiritual being may take hold of the body and use it as a means of expression. This is the first instance of taking hold of the body. How does it function and how does the loving attention in the environment affect the child?

Let us start with a phenomenological approach. What do we see? We look at the child, focus on the eyes and meet its gaze. We smile at the child and it smiles back. It sees us walking upright on two feet and it stands up; it hears us speak and begins to speak itself. We think while we speak, and the child begins to think. Doubtless these factors which have influenced the child are of a soul nature, even if they appear to reach the child through sense perception. However, the child gets hold of the meaning of the words and their grammatical form not through sense perception of the sounds, *not* through hearing them, although its sense perception is very different from that of an adult. Even being smiled at has a soul significance for the child which is difficult or actually impossible to put into words.

The following quotation about the nature of the human being comes from ancient Orphic mystery knowledge: I am child of the earth and of the starry heavens.

Theme for contemplation:

9. How does the child imitate? Does it observe what it imitates? Does it imitate only what it can observe with the senses?

5.
Imitating

The aptitude to imitate must be innate in the child; it does not 'learn' it and we cannot teach it to do it. Imitating cannot be taught, so the one being taught must already know what imitating is. The inborn aptitude is appealed to through soul/spiritual influences such as attention and love. The aptitude is brought from the world where the soul/spiritual being of the child was before birth or conception: the spiritual world of meanings and ego beings. It is definitely no material world, as meanings are free of material substance.

A baby can imitate, but it does not do so with intention. It does not resolve to do so; indeed, most imitated movements or functions do not happen consciously at all. For example, let us take the imitation of sounds or pitch, which is a capacity retained by adults from their childhood: We hear something through our ears, and our vocal cords or speech organs can reproduce straight away what they have heard — in the realm of speech and song we remain children. What causes the speech organs and vocal cords to know how to reproduce what they have heard? A likely explanation is that the organs in question accompany silently what is being heard and therefore a stream of air can possibly turn it into sound. The problem remains essentially the same even though it shifts a little if we ask: how do these organs know the way we participate during hearing? Bodily participation in the movements of expression always occur unconsciously,[15] yet this does not explain *how* it occurs.

But this superconscious way of working certainly points

to a spiritual origin of these capacities. In chapter 2 we tried to show in how far the child brings with it at birth an affinity to the character of earth existence — namely the fact that it consists of signs and meanings. We shall now turn to presenting existence in the spiritual realm, as it appears to us on the foundation of spiritual research and as it appears to us through logical deduction from an observation of earthly human beings. This will enable us to understand the nature and origin of 'imitating'.

Theme for meditation:
5. To understand is to imitate.

6.
Existence in the spiritual world

The main characteristic of human existence on earth today is our state of separation—from the spiritual world, from nature, from one another. The causes of this separation are obviously the material substance that the sense perceptible world of signs consists of, brain-bound thinking, our egoistic feeling of self, which is based on the body, and the non-communicative functioning of the body.

Material substance has a separating effect because it is spatial; and so does brain-bound thinking because the brain, like the whole body, belongs to a human being, and so do the non-communicative functions of the body such as for example the whole metabolism.

If we consider where and under what circumstances an unseparated human existence is to be found we arrive at three possibilities: in babies, in people of archaic cultures and in certain people who are handicapped, e.g. are autistic from their childhood onwards. In all these examples there is a lack of two of the potential causes of separation that were mentioned: the feeling of self or the egoity, and—in all probability—brain-bound thinking. Where babies are concerned the feeling of self appears one-and-a-half to three years after they are born. It is evident from the fact that the child begins to speak in the first person. In this period the brain is structured by the functions of consciousness—the speech centres by speaking, etc.

In ancient cultures or in what is left of them today, we see the sort of people whose consciousness, for the most part at least, is joined together by a group soul or, in other words, a common consciousness. As self-interest was not the guiding force in life then, ideally, everything had ritualistic character and 'religious' significance, if not in our sense. Along with self-interest, egoity — a strong feeling of self — was also ruled out. Feeling still has a predominantly perceptive character, and people therefore also have a successful relationship to nature without analytical science simply by following their feelings.

Since the start of assisted communication we know that people with severe autism on the one hand hardly feel their bodies, whilst on the other hand they feel their way extremely stongly into the thoughts and feelings in their surroundings. Where feeling is perceptive a person hardly needs thinking, and brain-bound thinking far less.

So we can ascertain that it is the feeling of self which brings about separation. That is the reason why direct, i.e. signless, communication stops functioning, because the greater part of the forces previously feeling their way perceptively into the environment now form a sheath for the person's feeling of self. This spreads itself around the body, though not in a spatial sense, and the inner part of the body now becomes sensitive if an inner organ is not functioning properly.

The acquisition of a feeling of self is like a repetition of the Fall that almost all traditions speak of, even if the form of the reports varies. Separation is a necessary cosmic impulse to make possible the human being's development of freedom and creativity, a freedom from the spiritual world.

In the spiritual world — the world of ego beings, from where the human spirit/soul is born on earth — there is no separation. It is a state of constant communication,[16] which is its very existence. In this existence we *are* conversation (Hölderlin), language, speaking, saying something without words, primeval existence. What this existence becomes on earth is the capacity to understand and communicate. We come from a world of understanding and communication, and what on this earth is a twofold faculty is one and the same in the spiritual world. In the same way as here on earth we give form to a statue, we ourselves are given form, and we ray out the meaning we have been given in the same way as a statue does. In this world there is no antipathy, only sympathy, in fact not as soul stirrings but as forces of dedication or division. In earth life spiritual sympathy comes over as understanding, knowing, perceiving: as identifying with something. For just as in the spiritual world we become the very thing of which we have been given the form, in earthly life we become, in the course of understanding, knowing and perceiving, for a homeopathically short moment, the very thing we are experiencing, thus identifying with it, and in the next moment, when we have disengaged ourselves from identifying with it, it immediately becomes our object. The essence of our attentiveness is this ability to identify, this dedication or love — and this is a reflection of spiritual existence. If the attentiveness is sufficiently intense and concentrated then it — and this includes us ourselves — becomes tangibly identical with what it is focused on. This is what happens in the theatre, in a concert — music is not an object — or in a concentration exercise, in meditation.[17]

Theme for contemplation:

10. If the feeling of self separates us from the realm of intuition, from intuitive thinking, we are left with rationality. Where could this acquire reliable orientation?

Themes for meditation:
6. Existence is communication without signs.
7. Attentiveness is love.

7.
Being given form

A baby's 'imitating' is actually an acquiring of form, which is a capacity it brings with it from prebirth existence, and which is even found in adults, namely in the limited realm of speaking and singing. When we hear, our speech organs or vocal cords are formed by what we hear and, as with a baby, this reaches right into the physical, whereas other formative influences only mould our attentiveness. In the course of every experience we have, this attentiveness becomes *the very thing* that we, indeed that our attentiveness is experiencing. Without noticing it, *we experience in everything that happens to us the metamorphosis of attentiveness into the theme in question.* This is why we arrive at the mistaken opinion that we experienced something which 'exists' independently of us.[18] For us to experience something—whether it be a thought, a feeling, a sense perception, a memory image or fantasy, it has to appear in our attentiveness. Anything that does not reach our attentiveness in some way—and this can be by hearing about it from someone else—we cannot know about. Even something we accept as a hypothesis, or fantasize about, must acquire form in our attentiveness. Thomas Aquinas called what we experience an image of cognition. If human beings consisted entirely of attentiveness we would be as we are in our prebirth condition, namely infinitely impressionable, malleable. For this very reason we would not *experience* being formed. For in order to be aware of something we need some firm point which is not included in the forming, and which affords the necessary withdrawal so that the forming can be witnessed from a point or a 'point of view' where no forming is taking place. To acquire such an anchorage was why human beings were furnished on earth with a body that is part mineral and part more mobile elements, which mediate between the soul/spiritual subject and the physical/mineral body, such as the sentient body (manifesting in the vegetative nervous system) and the etheric body which brings about the life of the organism and growth according to its proper form.

The further the spiritual part of a human being unites with the formed 'bodily sheaths' the less it can follow the shaping. This uniting occurs largely through the formation of the feeling of self in the body. This restricts the realm of experience so that adults become insensitive to a large part of reality. For instance they do not perceive immediately whether something is alive or not, nor do they have direct perception of the feeling reality of another being, and they need sense perceptible signs to communicate with their own kind. That this is not the case with a baby will be presented in greater detail in the chapter on acquiring speech.

Through the fact that the organism human beings are bound to has a more or less firm, uninvolved anchor — this becomes quite obvious through the feeling for self (chapter 11) — it lies in their power to reproduce the form impressed upon them, either to bring it to expression themselves or not to do so. That is the basis of their freedom. Because they have acquired this 'counterweight' or 'point of inertia' by means of a process which is called the Fall in every tradition worth mentioning, we can see why this Fall from the creator God was permitted, in fact prepared for.[19]

When we look once again at the miracle of the ability to imitate in the realm of speech we discover that it can disclose to us the nature of small children. We hear something, a sound complex, through our ears, yet the form-bringing principle affects the speech organs. This phenomenon can hardly be explained rationally. However, we can grasp it as a reminiscence of the prebirth state, where forming is at the same time reproducing. The forming has not happened by way of a physically perceptible process, as happens with sounds that are heard, but partly spiritually through immediate, direct communication; the perceiving and the reproducing 'organ' were one and the same, as though hearing and speaking were happening by way of the very same organ. On earth the passively perceiving organ has separated from the active organ. Therefore reproducing does not happen inevitably or involuntarily.

We are in the position to let what we hear sound forth although it has no similarity with the movement of the speech organs. Nor, when we hear something, do we see what the speaker's speech organs are doing. And even when we imitate an arm or hand movement it is a small miracle, because there, too, we do not perceive the mechanism of the movement: we do not see what either the muscles or the nerves are doing, and yet we are immediately capable of imitating the movement. In every case the imitating takes place by way of visualizing. We picture what we hear or see almost at the same moment as we perform it — though somewhat sooner in principle — and this is how the speech organs, vocal cords or limbs are 'informed' of what to do. However, it remains totally unclear from the physiological/physical point of view how the visualization influences the physical organs. Even when we ourselves speak, sing or perform a gesture we visualize the sound picture or the visual picture — and these visualizations have no similarity to the processes in the corresponding organs. Nor can this ability to imitate or reproduce be referred back to any kind of learning process, for a baby can imitate immediately with the accuracy with which it perceives. A good speech therapist does not correct the speaking of a wrong sound but the hearing of it. If a sound is heard properly then it can be made to sound right. Adults, too, can immediately reproduce sounds and sound complexes they have never heard or spoken before.

Our speech organs seem to be nearest to our consciousness. Just as in the prebirth state 'forming' is at the same time 'expression', where a baby is concerned speaking begins with imitating; then consciousness emancipates itself, becomes independent and begins to speak of its own accord.[20] We could say that we hear not only with our ears but also with our speech organs.

All the gestures of human consciousness — thinking, knowing, remembering, etc. — have their roots in an identity, a oneness with everything and everyone through identification, imitation, attentiveness and love. And what we call hope — including Thomas Aquinas' hope that in the future we shall know everything that is now the content of our belief — is founded on the fact that we do not become separate from one another for ever, but that at the end of time oneness will be restored again, and we shall be reunited with everything and everyone without giving up our uniqueness. The meditation for this insight is 'God is love' (1 John 4,8). But we have to go through the experience of hopelessness and forget this promise for a while. However, the 'never again' with regard to human encounters just does not exist.

Do you sometimes experience yourself as being one with the world? And at other times as being outside it, observing the world?

Theme for meditation:
8. Reproducing is part and parcel of hearing.

8.
The senses

Each particular sense realm arises out of an archetypal sense, which is the whole human being as baby with its impressionable nature. We could identify the archetypal sense as an all-inclusive attentiveness not yet split into specific sense realms and call it reversed will.[21] It still contains, as a unity, what will later divide into perceptive feeling and thinking. As long as the archetypal sense alone is active the human being cannot distinguish between the activities of the different senses, which means that at this stage of its development a baby cannot distinguish between hearing, seeing and tasting, for everything mingles as a willed feeling, a feeling will. The archetypal sense is normally 'instructed' by the environment out of which will activities of varying kinds come, and which gradually differentiate the receptive will. People could live even if not all the senses were working, and individuals born blind do not suffer from the lack, for the archetypal sense works all the time through all the different sense realms and can replace a missing sense, in some cases two. This was the situation with Helen Keller. She had meningitis at the age of nineteen months, leaving her deaf and blind; and yet she studied and became a successful authoress and speaker – a full human being.

The area in which the different senses operate arises through selective restricting of the attentiveness which at the beginning of life perceived universally as the archetypal sense. A baby 'learns' to distinguish between the different senses as its attentiveness concentrates selectively on one sense and cuts out the impressions from the other senses. This is necessary so as to differentiate between the senses, for the given world of perceptions speaks very seldom to one sense only.

How does the hearing of sounds arise? First of all hearing itself has to be separated out from archetypal perceiving—the impressionable will and universal feeling; general, comprehensive, unstructured attentiveness is split up and one part is selectively narrowed down to hearing. The word sense arises through a further restriction within the sense of hearing. The child 'learns' from the quality of voice to disregard the speaking person and to pay attention solely to *what* is being spoken, namely the specific form of the words. This instruction, which is selective attentiveness within hearing, can be called the word sense. To begin with the child hears words not sounds. The grasping of sounds is actually the outcome of an analytical observation of the word and arose at the same time as writing with letters, i.e. relatively late. Similarly the theories on sounds and letters (cabbala and the theory of Sanskrit on the 51 sounds) arose around the tenth century.

The sense of thought arises by way of further instruction of the attentiveness: The child learns to disregard the single words in a certain way and to pay attention to the meaning of the sentence. This again is a selective restricting of the attentiveness. How the child learns to 'understand' the meaning of the words is described in the next chapter. To start with the child thinks in sentences. The sentence, even if it consists of only one single word or sound, is the archetypal oneness of language. It is the essence of what is to be said. In so far as the child thinks, it thinks to begin with in its mother tongue. At this age the thought sense and the speech sense are still a unity and the dividing of them is probably one of the last stages in the formation of the different areas of the senses. After this the various senses are possibly trained for the different arts or even sciences, through a similar restricting process as with the senses in general. Accordingly, a sense is attentiveness that has been instructed and restricted, and it is an organ which is pervious and sensitive solely to the selected quality which has arisen through a process of restriction. After instruction the particular sense responds to what it is being taught, and when a new element occurs (e.g. if a person's sense of thought encounters a new thought for the first time) then the sense has to be taught this through an active effort at knowing (this new thought has first to be understood in thinking).

Theme for contemplation:

11. Which senses do we know of, if by sense we understand a function through which contents of consciousness can arise without any actual activity of understanding?

Theme for meditation:

9. Attentiveness has neither substance nor form.

9.
Acquiring speech

We described in the previous chapter the way the child acquires the sign aspect of language. Not less puzzling – yet it can be established by spiritual scientific research – is how it finds and applies the meaning of the first few hundred words or the implicit grammar in speaking them, without being able to think in the way an adult does.

At the start one cannot explain the meanings – and never does so, because on the one hand the child would not understand the explanations, and on the other hand there are a great many words in language that one could not explain at all (e.g. 'but'). 'Pointing' does not help here either. The pointing gesture was described by Augustine as the basis of word understanding – and in this respect the man whose thinking was otherwise so profound and sharp made a huge mistake. This view has often been taken up again since then. But it is fundamentally wrong. Firstly it presupposes that the child understands the pointing gesture, meaning that it has to look in the direction of the pointing finger, and secondly that it has an inkling of what is being pointed at. If, for instance, we point to a round, brown, wooden table with a smooth surface, the child should know whether we are pointing to the circular shape, the smoothness, the colour, the wood or the whole table. There are also a lot of words which we just cannot point to at all, such as conjunctions, adverbs, many adjectives, words which relate to processes of consciousness, and so on, such as 'although', 'now', 'nice', 'understand', etc.

In the speaker the meaning of the sentences and words is

a reality with the aid of which the person finds the words and the grammatical expression—the first thing in a sentence. This reality is directly and immediately accessible to the child through its perceptive feeling ('primal communication'). Its receptive attentiveness reaches to the language intentions of the speaker.

In this respect the child's path is the opposite of that of an adult. A sentence can be pictured like this:

The wordless meaning beyond language

The child's way　　　　　　　　　　　　*The adult's way*

Words

The adult arrives through an understanding of the words at the meaning of the sentence which is above the level of words. It is what translators have to find in 'no man's land' to be able to convey the meaning of what they are translating. A child understands the meaning of a phrase through signless primal communication, and arrives through this meaning at a meaning of the individual words. The faculty of soundless, signless primal communication originates, as we have said, in the prebirth realm. Nowadays this plays a big role in adults' conversation too: otherwise we would hardly be able to understand a new thought encountering us in the form of well-known words, but which are being used in a new sense.

As adults we easily let words sound forth without a corresponding experience. We say love, feeling, danger, without experiencing what we are saying: the words replace the experiences by just indicating them. With a little child these words and sentences include the experience of their content—this experience is of course the understanding of the text. To be attuned to the meaning is an ability we bring with us out of the prebirth realm; through the influence our environment has on us this becomes a specific ability for speaking. There is intention, i.e. will, at the basis of any kind of speech. In this original will, as though dissolved and hidden in it, is the content of the speech and also the feeling which is steered by the movement and functioning of the speech organs, without the entering in of ordinary day consciousness. The child is directly aware of this will in the speaker, and *this* is the experience we were referring to. The will of the other becomes the child's own will and brings about the corresponding movement of the speech organs and also the understanding. There is no other way we can explain how the speech organs know what they have to do to reproduce what they hear. The receptive reversed will turns the other person's will into the child's own. Both in the speaker as well as in the listener this will and the 'impression' it makes are unconscious.

So the small child's understanding is not at all a matter of thinking but rather of the reversed, receptive will or feeling, and the way to thinking is through them. A child's thinking is not the same as an adult's either; it is much more alive and shot through with feeling, and its character is experiential and not of the past. This kind of thinking produces structures in the brain, whilst an adult's ordinary thinking uses the same structures both as a supportive framework and as a mirroring surface; it uses them for thinking that is not intuitive and is also itself influenced by them. Adults can only carry out new, intuitive thinking by working *against* the existing structures. The first steps in thinking, as well as the first steps in speaking, still occur without the structures that will be used later: it is these attempts that create them in the first place.

Have you ever experienced a wordless understanding with another person?

Theme for contemplation:
12. What is the prerequisite for comparing different languages and/or for describing their grammar?

Themes for meditation:
10. We can only communicate meaning.
11. To be able to confirm that something is meaningless we must know what 'meaningful' means.

10.
The forming of concepts

When, in referring to the small child, we speak of an irradiation of formative will, the expression 'will' is a translation of a corresponding reality into something human beings are familiar with, but this is already a compromise, as we do not have a word for that communicating, meaningful reality. The word 'will' can only be given as a kind of indication of what this irradiation at the prebirth stage actually is. This irradiation is anyway differentiated, and as a light being—a communicative force—it shapes the recipient so that it develops organs according to the differentiated nature of the irradiation. Thus the realms of the senses come about, first of all the archetypal sense, a 'feeling' (the expression is just as inexact as the word 'will').

The realms of the senses gradually separate.[22] As these arise the mother tongues play a great part in their perception of quality, as they give the sense realms a definitely different structure.[23]

For the giving of shape to become possible there must be, as we already mentioned, some resistance to it, something that is itself not involved in the shaping: Then the interval between being shaped and not being shaped is experienced. This anchor is given to a human being in the form of his organism with which his spirit/soul partly identifies.[24] In this way there is an anchor and therefore an awareness of the experience. Through inner schooling a person can learn to replace the given bodily anchor with another one consisting of attentiveness itself.

If the 'reversed will' is a name for the understanding

receptivity to being shaped or the receiving being, then we can say that with increased resistance feeling arises out of this being. Feeling is much more conscious than the taking on of shape. If resistance grows even stronger then thinking arises out of feeling, namely receptive thinking, which we can also call intuitive, and which is active in forming concepts. Everyday thinking works with the concepts which are already completed, passes from one to the other, thus linking them together.

Thinking itself — which cannot be experienced by our everyday consciousness — is a continuity. Where this is interrupted, where thinking comes to a standstill, a concept arises. Concepts have a history, in the course of the evolution of consciousness they become more and more 'cramped' and restricted, but sharper, more precise in consequence. A small child's speaking and thinking in language comes about out of the need to communicate with adults — who have already lost the ability to communicate directly. The discontinuity of thinking is induced by mother tongues — every human language is discontinuous, consisting of separate words and sentences. Thinking crystallizes around and by means of signs, and in this way solid bodies take shape in the flow of thinking, bodies which are perhaps half solid to start with, single, jellylike particles, and these at least separate off out of the fluid. These formations are already of a conceptual nature, but much broader, far 'wider' in meaning than those of today's adults.[25] They are also far more indistinct. They structure the outer and the inner world differently according to the particular language, as both the vocabulary and the grammar of the various languages are different; also with regard to the inner world the structuring depends to start with on the language. The words 'nevertheless', 'whatsoever', and 'yet' can hardly be reproduced in other languages. We know that what little children get hold of first are the generic terms, the basic concepts. The name of the first animal they encounter represents 'animal'; if this is a cat then every animal is 'cat' for a while; the first colour they name stands for 'coloured', etc. But this is only part of the phenomenon, for these first concepts are still deeply immersed in a feeling specially belonging to them, out of which they emerge like a crystal out of a solution. In feeling there already are large fluidlike particles as a prelude to conceptual images into which they are continually transformed, just as the receptive will, feeling and thinking continually metamorphose into one another.[26]

Theme for contemplation:

13. How can we describe intuitive thinking as a process?

Themes for meditation:

12. Our concepts determine our perceptions.
13. What are 'facts'?

11.
The feeling of self

The existence, being and life of human beings after death or before birth is in a realm of comprehending, meaningful, meaningfully organized oneness with the world — the world of the created archetypes of creation (or nature), and the world of creative and comprehending ego beings. The memory, or what remains to us of this world in earthly life, is what we call meaning, communication, understanding. And speaking, knowing, remembering, and social interchange in a broad sense are based on what remains to us as a faculty from this spiritual existence. In acquiring speech — grasping the meaning of words and grammatical forms as well as 'imitating' the form of sounds — what is at work is the primal faculty brought from the undivided world.

The ego being starts taking hold of the body first of all through communicating gestures: eye contact and smiling, standing upright, speaking, and so on. Through willing feeling and feeling willing the still super-conscious ego being finds out from its fellow human being how the speech organs function, how a smile arises, and by reproducing these it at the same time grasps how it should function in its own body — although this is still not experienced as its own body. The meanings of the words and the grammar are grasped — super-consciously — through direct, signless communication. Up till then this all remains on the level of primal communication, and the baby who, to start with, experiences itself as existing in oneness with everything, is still not conscious of this.

The beginning of speaking in the first person marks a profound change, the start of stepping out and separating from communicative oneness, and at the same time it means a change in the child's relation to its body, which is now gradually felt to be its own. A sheath starts to form around the small child (but also within it) through which it begins to have a feeling of self, and this consists of the forces of feeling-knowing which were at work in primal communication and its continuation in the earthly world.[27] It is this sheath that cuts the child off from the world of primal communication and leads it into the dualistic world: I and the other. Later on this ego feeling can be observed, i.e. it can be the object of attentiveness, and this opens up the possibility of inner development towards the true self.[28]

To be able to experience something there has to be a force of consciousness present which identifies with what is to be experienced and at the same time can also be a resistance, a part of the attentiveness or awareness which does not identify with the act of knowing — and therefore is a witness to it. So that the organism as 'anchor' becomes an effective consciousness-bearing resistance, part of the force of attentiveness has to attach itself to the organism. This is the positive and essential role of the sheath of the feeling of self, which forms itself around the body (outside and inside). Otherwise human beings would stay in a state of being borne along in a dream.

To start with, the feeling of self is interpreted on the one hand as a bodily experience and on the other hand as an ego experience. In reality we are not aware of the body or of parts of the body but of the sentient sheath. This entity — usually called egoity — is brought about by two activities. One is the irradiation of the ego-imbued environment, which the child 'imitates', i.e. is formed by; the other is to be seen in that the child encounters situations, things, concepts and words which cannot, or can only with difficulty be understood by way of feeling. The baby's primal perceptive feeling cannot penetrate it. For example, if it experiences an adult flying into a temper: this does not lend itself to being communicated, and therefore comes across as senseless. The child's perceptive feeling cannot tackle it, bounces off, is rejected and, turned in on itself, it builds a form around itself which is closed off and is therefore no longer perceptive or communicative.[29] The same thing happens when the rage remains latent—for the small child cannot feel its way into the adult. There is a similar result when the child encounters anything that it cannot feel, or finds it difficult to do so, because it is not the expression of something that has sense but only self-interest. Before the coming into being of egoity the child does not understand what 'self-interest' means.

Thus there appears and grows in the child—and in the world—the by no means primal realm of non-communication. Communication in the dualistic world, which has arisen in this way, is an attempt to restore the oneness of primal communication.[30]

With the feeling of self the realm of what cannot be communicated comes on the scene—that is the nature of egoity—and takes over the human world as the principle of self interest.

Theme for contemplation:
14. What comes first, sign or meaning?

Theme for meditation:
14. How is the realm of signs connected with the realm of non-communication?

As long as the sheath of the feeling of self is not there a baby brings movement into its body on the one hand by way of the sentient body through reacting as it were to outer and inner perceptions (hunger, cold, bodily and soul states), and on the other hand in order to communicate (eye contact, smiling, stroking, and speaking, also in a non-verbal way). Through communicative gestures (standing upright and walking also belong here) the body is taken hold of by the spirit/soul without the feeling of self. The prototype of this first taking hold of the body is speaking. No bodily sensation accompanies this — we do not know how the speech organs move. In the case of these movements neither the sense of movement nor the sense of life function — they are controlled by the superconscious, without the participation of earthly consciousness. This is occupied with the content of what is spoken. The senses mentioned above (partly the sense of balance too) begin to function properly when the feeling of self comes into being. Then the person can perform intended, non-communicative movements. People in whom this sheath has not been properly developed do not have proper control of their body, they do not 'feel' it; there is even a lack or a reduction of a feeling for temperature or of pain, e.g. with people with severe autism and some other 'handicapped' people as well.

This feeling of self that we have — a feeling is observable, i.e. the *object* of attentiveness — is a human being's first form of ego consciousness. Steiner frequently calls it 'premature' because it is only a substitute for real ego-consciousness or self-awareness. This would be attentiveness experiencing itself and — if a person is developing in a healthy way — this can light up only around the twenty-first year. Usually, however, a person considers his feeling of self to be his ego being, a tragic mistake, which all spiritual traditions have fought against, just as they have all seen the development of the true ego as their most important goal.

There are people in whom the feeling of self is either weakly or not regularly developed (autists, children who are ADD and ADHD). If the sheath were missing altogether then we could expect to see the following symptoms:

— A lack of body awareness, a temporary or persistent incapacity to handle the body, especially difficulties with the motor functions.
— An openness to superconscious sources, creativity.
— An openness to other people, a perception of their thoughts and their feeling life without communicating by way of signs: 'clairaudience'.
— A weak centre of personality.

All these characterizations are often given regarding autism as well as other irregularities of soul/spiritual development. In fact autists often describe themselves in this way.[31]

When, in every day life, we move our hands and arms or, when doing gymnastics almost every part of our body, we can feel the participation of our sense of self, and this enables us to perceive the movement. Because we make a mental image of it we can carry it out through our sense of movement. This is how we get the impression that the parts of our body are being moved as though *from within* by this very sheath of self-feeling. We experience this differently in the case of movements of expression such as speaking, pointing, mimicry and smiling. When we carry these out we are not aware of ourselves, and we usually do not know, either, how we move that particular part of our body. When we look at our speaking (that is, afterwards), we ascertain that our speech organs are not moved by our conscious will but by what we intend to say — the content of our words—and that our attention is occupied with this content; therefore our feeling of self is not involved. So it is no exaggeration to say that our speech organs are moved as though *from outside*—and this is why there is no feeling and the sense of movement is silent too. When the sheath of self-feeling is not correspondingly developed, a present-day person has problems controlling his body, as we see in some cases of bodily handicap and autism.

We can ask at this point what the relationship between the spirit/soul and the body was like in archaic culture, when people did not speak in the first person, so that the egoity was either not active or only slightly, and the sheath of self-feeling had either not yet evolved or only to a small extent. We do know that these people could manage their bodies very well and skilfully, which today—disregarding the movements of expression—is hardly possible without this sheath.

The answer is to be found in the direction of these movements of expression. If, in a particular culture, the whole of life is sacramental, in other words meaningful, then every human activity, all bodily movements, are communicative, and serve to express something, and are therefore sparked off from outside; the body and its limbs are used as instruments, in which case it is obvious that in contrast to a movement of a hand or arm accompanied by a feeling of self, they are moved from outside. As, in the course of these old cultures and in the groups of people living in them, egoity gradually evolved, and in consequence the sacramental sense disappeared, movements as it were withdrew into the sheath of self-feeling and feel as though they are governed from within.

The archaic relation to the body or to parts of the body recurs in every artistic activity. When playing music, painting etc. the hands, arms, the whole body becomes an instrument, the feeling of self disappears, and in its place the active parts of the body grow together with the actual instrument (violin, bow, piano keys, paint brush, and so on) as though the sense of touch were being extended; for example with the piano, through the keys, the lever and hammer right up to the striking of the strings. In these cases this takes place without a feeling of self, the sense of touch working entirely towards the outside, as though knowing its way without, as with ordinary touching, activating the 'body feeling'. A similar transformation happens in the case of writing and certain types of sport. All these activities have first of all to be learnt consciously. Once these function then the described transformations occur. Moving our speech organs, carrying out facial expressions, also standing upright and walking, are normally not acquired consciously.

12.
Speech acquisition and the feeling of self

Human beings are born out of a world of direct — sign-less — communication, and on being born we remain for a long time in close contact with it. To start with a baby's awareness consists in feeling this connectedness. The connection remains, in a weakened form, and with inter-ruptions, for the rest of our lives, but we lose consciousness of it, and it thus becomes part of a superconscious being in which lies the source of our specifically human capacities. Earthly consciousness, the world of objects — and of the subject — begins the moment our conscious oneness — identity — with what we experience, ceases. With respect to our undivided consciousness we cannot actually speak of 'experience' at all, for what we have called 'resistance' or distance, has of course to be part of this. We have no expression for this kind of connection with the world — sometimes, though most unsuitably, called a 'participatory consciousness' in ethnology. A small child absorbs lan-guage, the meaning of sentences, words and grammatical forms whilst living in the world of oneness. With the forming of the self-feeling body this oneness is successively impaired to the same extent as this body becomes more and more impenetrable, until it is finally almost obliter-ated; and only in those special moments of intuition, of presence of mind, or of understanding, does it, mostly unnoticed, make a lightning appearance. As the child, right from the beginning, is surrounded by people who for the most part can only communicate through signs, it has to adapt itself to this kind of exchange.

In the process of 'adaptation' the remains of direct

communication and the arising feeling of self play an opposing role. The stronger the feeling of self becomes the less effective can be the undivided consciousness out of which the child draws its direct 'knowing' in regard to signs and their meaning. Originally signs and meaning are not separate at all—the child experiences the meaning together with the sign.

Children in whom the undivided consciousness echoes on for a long time are dreamy; we could call them Parsifal children, for that is how the young Parsifal is described. Their words and concepts still contain a great deal of the universal nature of primal meaning as used by people of earlier cultures, and their grammatical forms too. Children who use the first person early on are usually more awake, cleverer, and can speak and think like adults at an earlier age. This brightness is usually interrupted by periods of the old kind of consciousness, for instance when they are listening to fairytales. It is easy to observe in precocious children how the experience of a profound feeling for words changes into a reasoning cleverness. At the same time an endogenous fear arises in them which they project on to various outer circumstances. This—first—feeling of fear is the result of separating from oneness with the world, the loss of archetypal communication. Even a oneness with their environment ceases. Child psychology calls this the first phase of defiance. This fear—'archetypal fear', which arises simultaneously with egoity—concerns the body to begin with, and is a fear that something could happen to it. This has to do with the sheath of self-feeling which forms around the body, of course, and not with the body itself. This fear persists into adulthood, often in the form of not feeling well, which only on occasion turns to fear. Fear changes in an adult into being afraid of losing forms, fixations which are purely an emotional matter. In childhood and also in youth fear calls up attempts to restore oneness: by looking for love, striving for knowledge, forming groups, etc. By means of these goals the wound of separation can close over temporarily. If the feeling of self is too weak, then resistance, defiance and self-assertion will increase it, and cover up fear. Yet beneath the threshold of consciousness this behaviour will only encourage the growth of fear, and a vicious circle will arise: fear—defiance—fear.

In the age of the consciousness soul the possibility of breaking down this vicious circle alters for adults or young people after puberty. Everyone has in themselves the possibility of being creative, the 'second love', which brings into existence something that did not exist before. This is in accordance with the basic impulse of the Good with which a person is born. The adult's dualistic world picture is as it were defined by the structures of languages—meaning and sign. But experiencing the world as a duality only happens after the egoity has formed. Up till then the signs are perceived as being one with the meaning, so that both the speaker and the listener *experience* the sense or the meaning of the text together with the text. The prerequisite for this way of experiencing speech is that the sense enters the feeling simultaneously with the sign. There is no duality in feeling.

Perceptive feeling decreases in inverse proportion to the development of the feeling of self. That is the positive side of the sheath of self-feeling, that it partially separates the spirit/soul from out of the undivided world of the spirit providing it with provisional independence. With the arrival of the subconscious part, however, and an excessive increase in egoity, this independence is largely lost.

In chapter 6 we described life in the realm before birth or after death as a state of communication. It could just as well be characterized as a life of love or of sympathy. For communicating means giving another person your attention by way of the activity of speaking and listening. In the spiritual world the two earthly halves—speaking and listening—are still one; this is spiritual existence and, like feeling here on earth, knows no duality. It could also be called archetypal love. Its earthly reflection is 'first love' which strives to bridge the divide and in consequence becomes the driving force leading to communication also in the dualistic sphere, a communication by means of signs and meaning, expression and responsiveness. In contrast to this the feeling of self or egoity shows the opposite of love. It is uncommunicative, and in fact brings about separation by means of which it can appear as the first object our attentiveness encounters. All the other objects arise out of the primal separation. Love becomes self-love.

Its nature as an object is not recognized until later on, in the age of the consciousness soul. Egoity does not speak. It's nature is the opposite of communicative and it closes itself off from other people, keeps itself secret, gives nothing away, even misleads. For a long time humanity was ashamed of its egoity, regarding it as a result of the Fall, until, around the turn of the eighteenth to nineteenth century, it was legitimized in the economic theories of early capitalism (A. Smith and J. S. Mill), resulting in its being regarded as innate human nature.

Theme for contemplation:
15. Why do we need signs for communicating?

Theme for meditation:
15. Communication is love.

Summary

We can say that the child takes hold of its body in a twofold way by means of the forces which are released out of the inherited body and are at the disposal of the ego. The body is first of all taken hold of with the aid of the gestures of expression or of communication, such as eye contact, smiling, standing upright, walking and speaking. This happens by means of the gentle will, which means that the consciousness is engaged not with the bodily activity but with the content of the gesture of expression, and that the activity of the body or of part of the body proceeds without involving the feeling of self. Not until later, when the feeling of self or the egoity is developing, is the body, with the help of the sheath of self feeling, taken hold of by the hard will for the carrying out of non-communicative movements, and this will is always accompanied by bodily sensation by way of the sense of touch.[32] Every act of aggressiveness (hitting people, inflicting hurt on oneself, smashing things, causing damage, hurling things about, etc.) serves to give people a stronger feeling of self, of their own body. This shows clearly that the point where our attention is focused is where we experience ourselves.

In the case of severe autism even the first taking hold of the body in gestures of expression either does not happen or at least not with the normal intensity, and there is definitely a lack of the hard will (or, together with bodily feeling, it only occurs sporadically), and control of the body is in any case limited.

13.
A small child's spontaneous religiousness

The spiritual dimension of a human being is to be imagined thus: starting from the everyday consciousness it reaches up to the highest spiritual sphere but is only fully conscious on the plane of everyday consciousness. The specific human capacities such as thinking, knowing as such, intentional remembering, sensing and intuiting reach down at certain times — as though from above — into our awareness. At birth a baby's awareness sinks down fairly quickly, meaning that the upper parts of its spiritual being soon become superconscious, though its actual awareness does not correspond by a long way to that of an adult: a baby's spiritual being — the same as with people of an archaic culture — is still connected to the sphere of the archetypes, i.e. to the sense/meaning of things, of nature, of the material side of things. This means that its world of perception is hardly structured at all on the basis of concepts, or at least not to anything like the extent an adult's is. Perceiving, perceptive attentiveness, has to a large extent a feeling character. What appears by means of perception is the willing/feeling raying out of the perceived world. Because the child has no concepts for the world of perception it perceives the world with wonder and admiration. As the child perceives, the raying in of the world takes on qualities of feeling and will; these are neither subjective emotions nor memories or associations but *are* the actual beings of things felt in their reality. This kind of perception also impresses form on the body.

Immediately after birth the forces begin to be freed from the body. From the head system (which is chiefly localized in the head but spreads by way of the nerves over the whole body) forces of thinking and visualizing are freed, from the sentient body (represented by the vegetative nervous system) forces of knowing and feeling are freed, and from the physical body will forces are freed. Before becoming free these forces serve biological life and its regulation in accordance with perception.

Released from their original task they are then at the disposal of the human I and become active as forces of intelligence. They make it possible to learn and to be taught altogether, or we could say that they work as a small child's will forces. The world of perception, which to start with was in direct connection, as the world of meaning, with the child's spiritual being, now begins to work on the soul/spiritual being of the child through the freed forces and the sense organs and the developing sense realms. The effect of this spreads by way of the freed forces to the organism as well, because in the early years the process of becoming free has not yet finished: What happens with the forces works back on the biological life from which the forces came. In sleep, where they are more or less inte-grated into the organism again, they bring the various influences into it. Prior to this it was different: Until the age of one-and-a-half to three years the I has not yet identified with the body and the sheath of the feeling of self around the body. The child still speaks about its body in the third or the second person, for it has not 'slipped into it' yet. This I lives in perceiving and 'works' out from there, according to what it perceives, on the body, above all on the central nervous system, and through this—because it is still much more alive than in adulthood—on the whole body simul-taneously. The effect of the world of perception on the child seems to consist of this 'work' on the body, and the child is much more sensitive to that than in later life. This influence happens mostly not by way of the senses. The whole organism is still a sense organ, the primal organ — the organ of receptive feeling and the reversed, malleable will. This is formed by the universal will — in its basic nature. Every form, every quality rays out the kind of will out of which it has arisen and received its basic nature. Because the released forces are not totally independent they convey to the organism what they have been exposed to and what has formed them. The effect on the organism is lessened as perception increasingly takes place via the sense organs. The direct influence of the outer world decreases the more it in actual fact becomes 'outer world' by kindling physical, chemical processes in the sense organs and also electrical processes in the brain. This causes part of the irradiation to cease. For the role of the sense organs consists in toning down the irradiations, otherwise human beings would remain too dependent on them.[33]

We can conceive of the sense world (and also the supersensible world) as an irradiation of will[34] or as an influence on our feeling. Creations of art and natural beauty also work in this way on our feeling life. Everything that has form, also in the sense of having a quality, represents a will that has formed it or given it a quality. With regard to art and technology the formative will is not difficult to identify. Where an archaic consciousness is concerned, and also with respect to a baby in a certain phase of its development, things do not simply exist as such but are *happenings*, are processes (even a rock), and this process, the ongoing continuity of things, is preserved by a sustaining will. Augustine, Bonaventura and Thomas Aquinas call this will the will of God or the Trinity that 'sees' the world and lets the world be seen through the light which is the thing itself. This will or seeing has a speaking character and gives to both the archaic consciousness and the consciousness of children a content and feelings which cannot be put into words. In the course of the development of consciousness human sensitivity towards the will that sustains the world fades and eventually disappears altogether: things simply *are*—although the philosophical meaning of this kind of existence is not at all clear.

This will works on the 'imitating' child from outside through its receptive attentiveness, through the filter of individual choice. The effect concerns the whole organism, and the child at the same time grasps through its feeling attentiveness the 'meaning' of things, their speaking, their Logos character, although this could not be called 'knowing'. 'Knowing', 'religiousness', 'thinking', 'perceiving' and 'consciousness' etc. are categories that come to light through the consciousness soul's capacity to reflect. For these categories are only discoverable when human beings can look at their own consciousness and it's life.

If you could ask a baby or a person with archaic consciousness whether they are religious, whether they have 'faith', faith in the gods, they would not understand the question. For where a person of an archaic culture is concerned and partly where a baby is concerned too, the world is 'meaningful', contains and conveys meaning. The perceptible nature of the world is a sign of 'speech', i.e. a sign of meaning. And whenever speech, i.e. meaning appears, the unprejudiced soul assumes or knows naturally that there is 'someone' there, a person who is the source of the speaking, of the signs and meanings. The religiousness of archaic peoples (or what was *later* called religiousness) is seen in the fact that they see in the world a meaning and its source, i.e. someone who speaks. This seeing covers everything: Every perceptible thing, every process, every happening is a sign that has meaning, i.e. it can be read and understood. This is why every thing, process and happening is sacred, and holy—and has its existence as part of the whole creation, the fabric, the 'text' of signs and meanings. Thus the religiousness of a child and of an archaic person does not consist of thoughts or words, not even of feelings—they too would be different from everyday life. Where archaic consciousness (the ideal kind) is concerned, nothing profane, in our sense of the word, exists at all. And it would not exist for a child either, if the world of adults did nor confront it with the consciousness of a world they have made thoroughly profane.

A baby's attentiveness is directed towards the world it is presented with, and the child lives in 'imitation' under its spell which, seen from the point of view of the world, can be called its influence. At the time, the child entirely becomes *that* which it imitates, right into its bodily nature, and only later does it perceive it. The fact that it perceives means that there is a germinal subject there which remains independent in and of the perceiving. With a baby the source of speaking, the I, is still outside the organism and is aware of itself outside the organism (identifying itself with it roughly at the point where it starts saying 'I', which actually refers to an awareness of the body). This is why the child looks for the sources of the meanings of things belonging to the given world, its beings, 'outside', (outside itself), in fact it has no other possibility because its inner, conscious life does not begin until it says 'I' —until then the speaker also feels its own body to be 'outside' where the other things are. A baby is in its entirety a unity of spirit, soul and body. It is entirely a 'sense organ', and it lives in the unity of outer and inner will. When it *wills* it is *all* will, and there is no other thought or feeling which would influence its will: it is concentrated. The I does not yet have a 'life of its own' separate from the world, as occurs later when the child says I and the egoity is formed. The primal organ and the child as a whole are not yet selfish. In other words: The organism is still entirely an instrument of the spirit, mediated by the soul; one can say that it is an incomplete instrument that has not yet been entirely taken hold of by the spirit, the I. In so far as the I, the spirit, is active through the body — the activity does not arise in the biological realm, in the life of the organism, e.g. it is not a reflex movement — this activity has a sacred character, is a religious ceremony, i.e. is entirely an *expression* of the I, of the spirit in the sense world, a sign and just as sacred as the sense world itself is in its actuality.

In the lives of archaic peoples every alteration made by human beings in the natural course of things was carried out in this way: Agriculture, cattle breeding, house-building, crafts and cultural activities (script) all arose out of the religious cult. They began as religious and not simply useful activities and were made profane later. For archaic peoples and babies the world is a revelation. Sense perceptible things, appearing as they do as communicative will which points to its own source, have a religious aura: water, colours, plants are therefore holy, miraculous. Everything is of the nature of holiness, and of miracle: life, the world, existence. For today's babies this applies only with reservation. The difference between an archaic consciousness and that of a baby today is fairly large because nowadays babies live surrounded by adults whose consciousness has become considerably distant from ancient times. Therefore in the course of its development a baby very soon loses the feeling of holiness with regard to the surrounding things, and it only acquires this feeling in a rudimentary way, as soul/spiritual development in general mirrors the mentality of the environment, even if this varies from one individual to another. Thus we can state that nowadays a baby lives on the whole in two different kinds of consciousness. The first one mirrors the tendency to profanity living in the adult environment; the other one consists of the fairytale or 'religious' awareness which can be readily awakened in a small child. It is well-known how easily a little child finds its way into the world of fairytales, unless its imagination has not already been paralysed by television. A religious consciousness is very close to a child. And in fairytales every single thing, action or happening has 'meaning' corresponding exactly to the way it is in religious consciousness.

Although most grown-ups, too, like hearing good, well-told fairytales, which involves stepping out of their everyday consciousness, a fairytale consciousness very seldom takes hold of their whole being; and in the background their everyday consciousness lights up now and again. Although a fairytale consciousness is a refreshing relaxation they do not, as children do, take it absolutely seriously. Where children are concerned the world of fairytales is the element they actually relate to, and so they enter into them fully.

For the archaic consciousness and that of a small child it can reach the point where everything is given, even that which, for today's adults, arises only by means of their own activity, such as thinking or knowing. What today is observable as the process of knowing independent of an object or even of its subject was, for archaic consciousness, divided neither from its object nor its subject. The process of knowing was still one with the (later) object, the (later) subject, and this unity gave to the (known) world its holiness: it was a spiritual process in which the speaking will and the feeling of the world were still active and experienceable. 'Knowing' still belonged to the world — and this was why it was a light-filled world; at the same time a human being experienced the spiritual process—in so far as we can speak of 'experience' at all at this stage. It would be more correct to say: the spiritual process was also part of what was given, together with what later becomes the content of the spiritual process, of knowing. In this consciousness structure the fact of it being given belongs to the 'experience', in fact it plays the central role. The world, existence, is a gift—is given. This shade of feeling—the feeling of the world being presented as a gift—is nowadays almost totally lacking in adult feeling life, apart from the exceptional cases and situations when people, through illness for instance, have their ability to perceive restricted and then recover it fully. In that case a feeling of gratitude can awaken in them.[35]

In a child's spontaneous play the simplest object, the simplest happening, can acquire a religious character, if the player is really absorbed in the game. A leaf, a piece of wood, a pebble or sand can become an inexhaustible source of feeling, as long as rational thinking and perceiving do not predominate.

Theme for contemplation:
16. How does spontaneous religiousness arise and what brings it about?

Theme for meditation:
16. The simplicity of things is brought about by their meaning.

14

The I and the independent spiritual forces

The I is present in a human being right from the beginning; ego consciousness appearing normally between the ages of one-and-a-half and three. Before this point in time the ego is a superconscious capacity, namely one of attentiveness, which can be seen clearest of all in the acquiring of speaking and thinking. But even before this the ego has brought it about in a baby that it raises itself above the lying and crawling position, stands upright and starts to walk. Both 'achievements', from the aspect of physics, are incredible and take place, as also the phenomena of speaking and thinking, only in a human environment, where speaking and thinking are the norm. Even before these changes there are signs of an ego being, such as the first communicative gesture, eye contact, which is possible only between human beings. When we observe the inner gesture which also enables this to happen between adults, and compare this way of looking with that of an eye specialist—where the same movement has an altogether different character—we discover in these two ways of looking the two opposite forms of attentiveness, the receptive and the intentional kind. The latter focuses on a pre-determined object, while the former searches for the object, expects it and helps it into existence (e.g. in the case of a new thought). Eye contact comes about through the receptive gaze of both partners, and stops as soon as one of them thinks of something or the shadow of a self-centred wish enters the consciousness. This is why eye contact between adults seldom lasts long, in fact there are more and more people who are either not capable of it or not willing to experience it. The look, the glance in eye contact, has no definite goal, no particular object (as for instance the colour of the eyes), but is directed at the glance of the other ego being, and the look *happens, arises,* is continuously *created,* and does not just *exist.*

The second communicative gesture of the I is smiling. A few weeks after birth (but earlier and earlier in our time), after the first eye contact, the child smiles back when it has been smiled at — an exclusively human trait.

By way of these phenomena just mentioned the organism is taken hold of more and more by the ego and clearly used as an expression of the I. This — our human attentiveness — is tuned to sense and meaning. This is what brings about the connection between sign and meaning, a connection which to a large extent is non-mechanical. This is the foundation for the capacity to be taught and to be able to learn. These capacities are neither secondary reflexes nor forms of behaviour, nor are they acquired in a similar manner.

In the animal realm, forms of behaviour and reflexes, also the secondary ones, always serve to maintain physical life; whereas in human beings their attentiveness, their dedication, (deep, self-forgetful attentiveness) is independent of biological aspects. Soon after its birth a baby retains only very few reflexes and as good as no biologically useful instincts. What we sometimes call 'lower instincts' in adults are not material ones but a secondary appearance, and they usually work counter to health (e.g. smoking).

When we compare human beings to animals (the higher mammals) the difference by way of attentiveness and its bearing on the way we do things is obvious:

a) Human attentiveness can deviate from biological requirements, whereas that of an animal cannot do so,

except perhaps in a young animal and apparently as
the result of training.

b)   In the case of human beings there is usually a moment
of reflection between perceiving and acting; in animals
a particular perception sets off a particular action or, as
the case may be, prevents it.

c)   Human attentiveness can focus on biological processes,
on the facts and questions of existence, on philosophy
and art and the pleasures that can be realized by means
of biological processes: with animals their 'attentiveness' is determined practically by biological needs and
things associated with them, governed by wise
instincts which serve life. Human beings lack these
altogether. Human attentiveness and behaviour are on
the whole free (or could be free), with animals these are
determined by their species and the circumstances (e.g.
the season of the year). The difference is clearly seen in
communication and its elaboration. Animal sounds are
inherited, not learnt, the mother tongue of human
beings is determined solely by the environment, and it
also depends on this whether they learn to speak at all.
By considering such things it can become quite clear
that in a human being a living, feeling organism is
connected to a — potentially — totally free spiritual
being. After birth this being takes hold of the organism
more and more strongly and works to make use of it as
an instrument of expression. Speaking is clearly the
fundamental, central means of expressing oneself. The
activity of the I as spiritual being is in this case
represented by the intention in the speaking, the
meaning factor, whilst the role of the organism is
presented in the movement of the speech organs; the
working together of these two parts is a perfect
example of the associating of I and organism.

The movements that serve speech, and human movements in general are, in contrast to animal movements, not instinctive. In the animal realm it is the sentient body that controls the instinctive movements, and it is this that reacts to the perceived environment and the state of the organism (e.g. hunger). This sentient body has a different form of behaviour and reaction all according to the particular animal species. Apart from the sentient body a human being also has a sentient soul which consists of all the forces of the sentient body that become free in the course of a lifetime. The sentient soul is the first manifestation of the conscious I. Therefore the sentient body only plays a small part in the life of human beings compared to that of animals. In the latter case their sentient body is bound up with their whole natural surroundings, it engenders a feeling response, causes the animal to act and controls its activity. For example chamois do not need to pay attention to what their legs are doing when they race down a scree-covered slope—nor would they have the time to do so. In human beings the sentient body is not bound up with nature as a whole but with the sentient soul. This consists, as we said, of similar forces to that of the sentient body, only they are not formed and they do not dictate a certain behaviour. The forces of feeling which become free in a baby are those of 'imitation'. In contrast to the forces of the sentient body these can, in imitating, assume any form. Therefore from a certain point of view they can be regarded as forces of knowledge. In acquiring knowledge the respective forces (of thinking, feeling and will) take on the form corresponding to the particular thing becoming known. They are not formed to endure, i.e. they do not become forces of habit. For instance the forces of thinking can sometimes assume the form of one thought and then let go of it again to take on the form of another thought. The free forces of feeling can—determined by the ego super-consciously—regulate the movement of the speech organs. As perceptive (i.e. free) feeling still contains dissolved in it so to speak what will later on separate out as thinking, the content (meaning) of what is spoken in the environment is also accessible to 'imitation'. The free forces of the sentient soul mediate the impulses of the ego, as originally they were released from the sentient body by the ego. They are at the disposal of the ego.

The free feeling forces are used in the movements of the body. At the same time they perceive the form of movement determined by the sense of movement. The latter conveys to us, also by way of the free forces, what kind of movement we are doing with our hands or feet, without our having to look. This is obvious actually, for all we would see if we looked would be the completed movement. The form of it, however, would have to be prescribed before it was carried out: and this is the function of the sense of movement. Since human beings can as good as do any movement (e.g. with their hands), the forces at work in the sense of movement must be totally free, not tied to form and controlled by the ego. Movements of expression, like those of the speech organs, are neither planned, i.e. visualized, nor carried out consciously, but occur uncon-sciously, outside the jurisdiction of the sense of movement.

In our movements the free life forces work together with the free forces of feeling. These life forces are the growth forces of biological life yet, in contrast to the physical forces, they also determine the *form* of growth, the structure of the organs. Therefore they can be called forces of form. With animals, besides growth, these are also responsible for movements which are controlled by the inherited pat-terns of feeling-perception in the sentient body. With human beings, free life forces and feeling forces must already be available when the child learns to talk, to enable the speech organs to be capable of executing the required highly complicated movements, which are not inherited. The life forces released from biological functions are just as form-free as the feeling forces which have become free in the sentient body. This is how a human being becomes capable of acquiring any system of speech sounds and reproducing it.

As the form forces are released step by step vitality continuously decreases with age, as can be seen for instance in the slowing down of the healing of wounds.

The release of the sentient and life forces is a process that is continuously at work from birth to death, but which roughly every seven years shows a kind of nodal point or milestone (change of teeth, puberty.) We can conclude from the change of teeth that the child is ready to go to school. The forces of form which have created the second teeth become free and are now at the disposal of the intelligence. Education works with the free feeling forces and the life forces through the I, whereas training makes use of the forms of behaviour and of reaction bound up with the biological forces to produce secondary instinctive reflex forms.

Just as in bringing speaking to physical realization the I moves the speech organs, superconsciously, with the help of the independent sentient and life forces, where artistic activities are concerned it is chiefly through conscious learning and practice that the hands or the whole body become speech organs: Once the artistic ability has been acquired the consciousness is of course only occupied with content (i.e. with the musical 'message') and not with moving the corresponding parts of the body. Because with artistic activity the feeling (not thinking) meaning is the decisive thing, so that feeling and thinking also co-operate with the will to express something,[36] an activity of this kind both in the soul life of the child and of the adult is therapeutic and health-maintaining, as it preserves or restores the original unity of will, feeling and thinking.

Through being attuned to meaning or sense the healthy, independent forces preserve the ability to enter into any form without being imprisoned in it. The formative forces working in biology produce a certain plant or vegetable or animal organ and keep it alive.

The I is human attentiveness. It is active both in the small child without being ego-conscious and in the adult in self-effacing devotion. Ego consciousness appears just when this devotional attitude is not present, in that part of the attentiveness which connects up with the feeling of the body. It is a sign of this connection when the child starts using the words 'I', 'me', 'my' etc. with reference to the body. This identification produces egoity and the sub-conscious formations connected with this, consisting of the independent forces which have fallen away from the ego, from free attentiveness. Egoity is attentiveness which is directed towards the feeling of the body and can no longer free itself from this. On the basis of the sheath of self-feeling uninformed soul forms arise such as vanity and envy. Because the ego, as inverted, receptive will or the will to express something, has first and foremost the character of will, the attentiveness that has become distorted and imprisoned in forms has control over part of the will. This is where such things arise as passion, addictions of all kinds, secondary instincts and those will forms aimed at serving a person's comfort and profit. These forms do not serve to maintain life and health but undermine them.

The ego-centred will is released from the physical body. In order to understand this we shall have to remember certain things. If a lifeless object (a table, statue) is given form, a formative will has been at work, an active will.[37] We can imagine it as continuing to preserve and maintain the form that has been produced, and this is actually how little children or archaic peoples perceive it. A lifeless object only changes (also chemically) by way of an outside influence. The plant, as it develops, alters its shape and size from out of itself: the formative will that controls growth is seated in the formative forces of life and works on the life of the plant all according to species. Change is also connected with its particular position, which the plant cannot alter by itself. Here, the will which forms the physical body of the plant is already free of the physical body. With animals there exists a species-orientated will controlling growth and also a species-orientated will controlling movement governed by the sentient body. This manifests in the kind of behaviour typical of a species. In human beings, in addition to the above-described types of will, we can also observe a free will that supports the respective ego-consciousness. The closer the physical body gets to attaining its 'finished' form the more its will forces become free.

Theme for contemplation:
17. What is it that stimulates human action?

Theme for meditation:
17. What is it that characterises the free will (or a free deed, a free action)?

15.
Star children and difficult children

Babies have always been strangers in the world of adults, as they come from a world in which existence is at the same time communicating, a kind of communication without signs, direct archetypal communication between beings whose essence is of the same nature as meaning, and this is what human spirits are prior to conception and birth. Just as the 'meanings' of sense-perceptible signs do not consist of material substance, neither do the beings who can understand or create meanings. Adults, on the other hand, live in a world of sense-perceptible signs, and for the most part they take them to be realities without recognizing their meaning, without even having an inkling that they symbolize meanings: the natural scientific view of the world. Child education used to consist and still mostly does consist of making children fit as quickly as possible into this world of signs and meanings, in which the meaning aspect is almost always assumed to be nominal. In past times this practice could succeed more or less, because remnants of wisdom from earlier, more spiritually-based traditions still played a part in education. A few decades ago this situation changed dramatically, however. The gap between the child and the world of adults is growing ever greater, and doing so with increasing speed. On the one hand children are increasingly being born with spiritual tendencies; on the other hand the adult world is getting further away, faster and faster, from spirituality: it is steeped in a purely materialistic mentality and way of life.

For roughly the past twenty years now (and occasionally well before that) more and more children are being born who are different—different from what parents and teachers are used to seeing and expect to see. For a long while these children were considered, and treated, as special cases, strange aberrations from 'normal' children. By the larger and ever-growing numbers we see today, it is clearly not a matter of individual cases, but that a new generation of souls we have never met before is coming to earth—children who have great maturity, are dissatisfied with the adult world as it is today, and are coming to earth with a powerful spiritual impulse. We cannot close our eyes to this event any longer.

The first and foremost thing that can strike parents at the children's birth is the very early eye contact—this usually happens immediately after birth. This cannot be attributed to the influence of the environment, the time is too short for that. And the look these new children give you—I suggest calling them 'star children'; in the USA they are usually called 'indigo children'—is not the look of a baby but of a mature, self-aware and wise person. We can tell the difference, surely, between a self-aware look and one that only 'looks out' at the world. Self-awareness in the gaze is something unmistakable. And we can see not only self-awareness in it but also dignity. Later on this will characterize the child's whole behaviour.

The gaze will reveal something else, too, if you learn to understand it: that the environment, that is, adults, are transparent to it. 'Seeing through' things is a capacity all babies have, but with star children an adult can perceive this ability in the child's look. This ability does not get lost later on, however; the child can also express later on what it 'sees' in the adult.

Right from the start these children have their own individual character which they champion very strongly—they know who they are. All children are becoming more and more individual, of course, as seen and reported by kindergarten teachers, school teachers and parents, but with star children this occurs with consciousness, consciousness of self. They know they are different from the 'normal' run, who still form the majority in schools and kindergartens; the 'new ones' unfailingly recognize one another and form groups together. If the teacher has not put himself in the picture the two types can easily antagonize one another. Star children speak very early in the first person without at the same time losing their extraordinary sensitivity, as is the case in this connection with 'normal' children. They continue to perceive everything in the adults and give early expression to what they have seen. They also, at an early age, and in no uncertain terms, say what they want and what they don't want. You cannot simply order them about but have to talk to them about what you intend. If you don't do this they will put up stubborn resistance — they want to be treated with respect. If you want them to do something, you have to talk it all over with them. A discussion is appropriate even if they are too young to have any understanding of what is being discussed, for in this case too it makes them feel appreciated and respected. And if there is a possible lack of 'intellectual' understanding this is often (also with mentally retarded people) replaced, as is well known, by a feeling understanding.

Despite their marked individual characteristics star children show soul/spiritual qualities in common which distinguish them from 'normal' children. These will make it impossible for an expert to misjudge the situation. Namely that we are perceiving an invasion not of 'science fiction beings' from other planets, but of human souls who, in a spiritual sense, have come of age. Having now reached maturity they are arriving from their own star — one that is not sense-perceptibly visible, but a star similar to the one that appeared to the three wise-men at the birth of Jesus, and led them on their way from Jerusalem to Bethlehem: the guiding star of a true, supersensible astrology.

We ought right from the beginning to treat these children differently, according to their maturity — mature but not precocious. Once the beginning has been spoilt and the environment or the teacher stick to their usual, conventional 'methods', it will become more and more difficult later on to deal with the growing child.

Where these children are concerned there exists no such thing as an authority depending on position (as parent or teacher) — and right from the start this is so, whilst they are still very small. On the other hand there is on their side an appreciation and love according to 'deserts'. With pretence you get nowhere — every lack of sincerity, any attempt to fake it is spotted as quick as lightning, rejected and despised. What are really appreciated are honesty, the admission of possible shortcomings or mistakes, and originality. They themselves are original and honest and stand no lies; dealing with them is direct and uncomplicated if you have won their confidence. They know for sure whom they can confide in and whom not. They disapprove of any proceedings done as a habit or ritual, and find new, usually more effective, ways to learn or proceed. You cannot punish them, for the punishment doesn't help, and leads at most to their rejecting from then on the person who set the punishment; it is taken as a sign of weakness, an incapacity to deal with them — which in fact it is. You cannot arouse a guilty conscience in them or feeling of shame — not from outside — as an 'educational' aid.

Star children usually have surplus vitality and mental energy which shows a similarity to children who are ill. They are often classified as having the syndromes ADD (attention deficit disorder) or ADHD (attention deficit hyperactive disorder). In actual fact, though, they only pay attention to something that really interests them, but then they can become strongly engrossed in it. If something doesn't interest them they easily become bored and get restless. It depends on the environment, on their teachers, whether an interest can be awakened in them for the subject or theme. If this is successful then the child will have no attention problems—nor will the teachers for their part have any problems with the child. But if it doesn't succeed then the child will become very restless and will hardly be got to concern itself at all with the object of the lesson.

These new children are usually highly intelligent, and in all kinds of intelligence tests they range far above the average in their age group—unless they adamantly refuse to be tested at all. But originality can hardly be tested.

They are very sensitive as well, in both directions: both concerning themselves and with regard to their fellows. If they have not already been 'spoilt' by the environment they show sincere compassion, and their actions are prompted by love—this is particularly noticeable. What upsets them most is experiencing that others are not prompted by love. As they are so sensitive they can do with an emotionally stable, secure adult environment, one that radiates security—a rarity. They easily become frustrated, often because they cannot put their many original ideas into practice. They suffer failure badly, which often produces a block, and then they relinquish their plan. Learning by heart, memorizing is not desirable; they like learning by experiencing things and experimenting. Not a few of them have spiritual experiences which they also discuss among themselves, and they are very interested in experiences of this kind. If they are not understood they withdraw, and are indignant if someone obviously acts without love. If there is someone who is ill or unhappy they quietly form a comforting circle around them, and usually achieve success — with no words spoken, nor do they make plans to do this beforehand.

They know that they themselves and also all other people are spiritual beings. They clearly 'see' the spiritual element in people, that is, they perceive its quality, and they take reincarnation for granted. They often seem to know what earlier incarnations they had — but as the thoughts and feelings of other people are accessible to them it is not easy to distinguish (especially in a New Age environment) what is their own experience and what are other people's thoughts. Every hidden intention and every secret thought lies open to these children. This ought to determine the basic nature of conduct in their environment.

What is known about star children could lead to a change of attitude in the adults in their environment, although knowing about something is not yet being able to do something about it. Adults certainly ought to acquire new abilities if they want to give the new generation a positive welcome. Without this, star children will, to begin with, be difficult children, and possibly addicts or criminals later on. They want to change the world through their spiritual impulses, give it forms springing from compassion and love. This will not succeed if the adult world, which they will inevitably come into contact with, does not change accordingly. Without inner change, through our very lack of understanding, and misunderstanding, we shall make the star children into broken people, shattered in their innermost being with regard to the mission with which they came to earth — we can hinder them in their mission to turn the world into a better place, rob them of the meaning of their existence. The great rejoicing with which these children are welcomed, with reason, in New Age circles, will prove to have been a vain expectation, if adults stick to their habits of doing nothing about their own spiritual development.

A way of dealing with star children will be described in chapter 23. However, we can already say what the two fundamental features of a suitable attitude are: respect and uncompromising honesty. Both features require that we work on ourselves. Honesty (also honest respect for the children themselves) demands profound self-knowledge. Whoever is not honest with themselves — and without inner schooling such honesty seldom occurs — cannot be sincere where other people are concerned either.

With star children the sheath of the feeling of self does not seem to be developed to the same extent as with 'normal' children, their self-awareness is not geared to their feeling of self. This is what gives them on the one side their intuitiveness and intelligence and on the other their loving attitude to others, as long as they have not been rejected in some way and driven into 'difficult' ways.

Nowadays intense spirituality on the one side and the intense practice (not theory) of materialism on the other are clashing with one another. The result is such a rapid and complex increase in the number of 'difficult' children that the 'experts' can hardly keep up with analysing the various typologies and syndromes. But it is more or less public knowledge that frustrated spirituality (creativity) turns to rebelliousness, behavioural disturbances, addiction and criminality, as well as mental and physical illnesses. That there are 'difficult' children, and what they can become should the occasion arise, is largely due to the way star children react if they have lost their mission, the meaning of their existence.

All small children still live to a large extent in the spiritual world before they can speak actively, (this is the 'autistic' stage of development) and they would have a great deal to tell us about this world if they were capable of it. But the reason why they cannot communicate through signs is because they still partly participate in spiritual experiences (direct communication). Some of them speak of this later, but what they tell is seldom accepted. Star children could be a source of insights into the life of babies before they speak, for they are later on not totally separated from these sources.

16.
The distinctiveness of star children

The 'star' is that spiritual part of a human being that remains in the spiritual world also during earthly life, becoming connected at birth with the body through attentiveness, the inner light. At the beginning of life the stream of attentiveness is homogeneous, uniform. When the sheath of the feeling of self is formed it is split into two: into a feeling component that can identify with everything, and into another which, as witness to this metamorphosis, can be called the I component. It is the first component out of which the ego body, the feeling of self as a closed form (sheath) is formed, as an addition to the inherited body; and it is due to this that the part of the original homogeneous stream of attentiveness acting as witness became independent. This is why generally speaking people can remember back to the time they first called themselves I—although there are plenty of exceptions.

The ego stream and the part of the feeling stream which has remained formfree consist of independent forces. These form the receptive part of the attentiveness that receives the 'gifts', the intuitions, the kernel of the creative ideas from the star, whilst the forces that have been released from the body are active in the realization of these ideas through the body (e.g. in the sounding of speech). The first form of ego consciousness arises as a rule through the fact that the feeling of self is taken to be the ego.

The soul/spiritual structure of star children is different from the general make-up of a human being in three main ways:

1. The sheath of the feeling of self is optimal, i.e. very thin, guaranteeing solely the possibility of bodily movements which are not movements of expression. Therefore the forming of egoity is for the most part omitted, and the loving part of the child's being continues to function even after saying I.
2. As the sheath of the feeling of self is weak the two components of the stream of attentiveness are not sharply or fundamentally separated, the connection to the star is not or is hardly interrupted.
3. Ego-consciousness or consciousness of self, which is so characteristic of these children, does not arise from the feeling of self but from the attentiveness that has remained strong, and which (as inner light) can experience itself in the vicinity of the star, thus becoming the self, the true I.

The weakly developed sheath of the feeling of self explains why these children have perceptive feeling enabling them to see through people and have access to their thoughts and emotions. Unlike 'normal' children, star children retain this ability as long as they do not become 'difficult'.

Repeated disappointment, the experience of not succeeding in realizing their intentions, the shock of being in an environment that pretends to be other than it is and which they can see through, and similar discoveries, can turn star children into difficult children, into little devils. Their sheath of self feeling probably becomes denser at the cost of the stream of attentiveness which has previously been independent. Due to the fact that when the sheath was first formed only a relatively small part of the feeling stream had participated, there is not a sharp or fundamental division of the two components of attentiveness. If further parts of the attentiveness now get caught up in the sheath, then the I stream that is not separated from the other one is involved in this, which is normally not the case: otherwise it is mostly only the feeling stream that is included in the 'senseless', non-communicative soul forms. The involvement of the testifying components puts children in an unapproachable state of annoyance and you cannot talk to them—any more than you can talk to adults when they are deeply entangled in an emotion such as anger.

Theme for contemplation:
18. What does coming of age really mean?

Theme for meditation:
18. Attentiveness is only now.

Advice prior to the practical part

Teachers and parents who have no option but to get involved with 'difficult' children—and we shall soon encounter no other kind of child—will find that none of the literature on anthropology, psychology, even spiritual scientific knowledge, although necessary to a certain extent—is much use to them, nor is it sufficient. For education pushed more and more towards therapeutic education can or could be effective only under the conditions that teachers train and increase their attentiveness until it becomes an ability to have spiritual experiences. This is the only way in which they can do justice to the child's individuality: through their own 'here and now' intuition, love and devotion, meaning attentiveness raised to an unlimited level, also in feeling and will, which become perceptive faculties. Schooling in consciousness and in attentiveness should be one of the chief subjects of teacher training. The big question is: Who is going to teach it? And we do not have to try to overreach ourselves: Concentrated attentiveness passes almost of its own accord into the capacity to perceive when the turning point, the spiritual I-experience, has been reached. Whereas with the aforesaid capacity one would be able to experience the individuality of the child, without this experience of the turning point, the only thing that works through the teacher is the egoistic self-feeling ego, whose inclinations and deeds rule and determine the world scene nowadays in the same way as do all the principles of self-interest that small children cannot understand because these things only make sense to them when the egoity has been formed — which is indicated by speaking in the first person.

What spiritual children actually require is a spiritual adult. If we are pessimistic in the face of this possibility (and there is sufficient cause for it) we can explain the general bankrupt state of the world.

The scene in families, kindergartens, schools and therapeutic education institutions today can be looked at as a *protest of the human soul*. There is a broad palette: It extends from children with speech and behavioural disturbances, through dyslexia, attention problems, hyperactivity, lack of interest, to autism. The majority today will perhaps accommodate themselves to the normal world of adults by adjusting, through outer or inner pressure (to avoid isolation and to obtain love from the environment); in the not far future this may well succeed less often and with greater difficulty. *And this is our hope.* Today we can still treat the childhood 'drop-outs' as abnormal creatures and push them into a corner of civilization; but with their growing numbers this will no longer be possible. The question is: Who will understand the protest? Who will restore to health this perverted creativity and originality? How can this primary impulse of a spiritual culture assert itself? (This last question has been dealt with deeply and pessimistically in Aldous Huxley's last novel *Island*.) At the least we should not misunderstand the spiritual impulse that is overtaking us and try not to channel it into civilization's dustbin.

II
PRACTICAL TRAINING

17.
Attentiveness

The more our attentiveness is free of form the deeper we shall reach with our knowing. A sick soul suffers from lack of attentiveness because large parts of the attentiveness are tied up in senseless, i.e. non-communicative forms.[38] The egoity or the feeling of self, for example, is this kind of form — the foundation of all the other non-communicative forms. These are predominantly feeling and will forms, but in the thinking too there are fixations or difficulties with regard to the lack of ability to get involved in new thoughts or trains of thought. Even healthy attentiveness does not move in an entirely formless way. It is well-known, for example, to what extent the mother tongue and the environment in which people grow up and are educated influences their manner of thinking or their feeling reactions. Our mode of thinking is a kind of form — even if it is somewhat blurred — and alone the fact that we use our thinking for knowing the 'given' world signifies a certain mould: that which is given is already given shape by concepts unconsciously available, unless the person acquiring knowledge consciously dissolves this form. If the style of the thinking approach is loosened, then the acquiring of knowledge can change from the thinking kind to that of feeling or even willing — the impressionable, receptive will.[39]

The aim of the teacher would be to get to know better and better the actual soul disposition of the child and the ego-being behind it in its various metamorphoses. What we need to know here are 'forms' one cannot describe in words, because they are more flowing, changeable and generous than forms one can describe. To give an analogy: It is impossible enough to describe a piece of music or a melody in words, but how much more impossible is it to describe the composer's style—although we can immediately recognize either one or the other. This tells us clearly that a composer's style is more formless than a piece of music or a melody of his. But style is all the same also a 'shaping' and can alter in the course of life: In principle the ego or the creative attentiveness is even freer.

As we have already explained: Whatever we get to know is a metamorphosis of our attentiveness, the thinking, feeling or willing kind, none of them ever working on their own, and each being capable of the greatest differentiation (e.g. in the perception of colour and taste). When attentiveness increases beyond the quality of will it becomes a kind of state of being. This can be called 'love' as it is directed towards unity and oneness. These qualities of attentiveness of the highest kind are described in the different traditions as 'emptiness', 'freedom from form', 'light', a state of being that transcends both existence and non-existence (in the usual sense). Without experiencing them the descriptions remain mere words and ideas which virtually distract from what they are indicating. In our knowing or experiencing our attentiveness assumes each time the form and quality of which we are acquiring knowledge and experience and which we designate as such. We know the change in our attentiveness as the image of cognition (Thomas Aquinas) and consider it to be *the* reality. The way we experience this can change if the ability to know it—the attentiveness at that specific moment—changes.

Well, everything we might know about a person is to a large extent 'formfree' in comparison to things. Therefore to get to know a child it is necessary to have a largely formfree attentiveness and to be able to recognize the unnameable qualities which are individual in every case. Coarse forms in attentiveness are for example preconception, prejudice, wishful thinking. Just dissolving forms such as these is not at all easy. Then it would be the turn of dissolving thinking in words,[40] the development of thinking that is above language; then the dissolution of given conceptual forms—a changing over to *concept-forming* 'thinking', to feeling knowing, etc. The more formed the attentiveness is the less it can enter into the forms one might be able to know. Exercises in attentiveness help to dissolve forms, especially the so-called concentration exercise (chapter 18).

Forms play an important role in the development of ego-consciousness. However, an ego-consciousness that indulges in forms is a soul consciousness; an ego-consciousness that is relatively formfree would be a spiritual ego-consciousness.[40A] A baby, as a soul/spiritual being, is initially hardly connected to the inherited body and still lives entirely in spirituality. Once the egoity has been formed, when it begins to speak in the first person, the ego-substance, the attentiveness, takes on the first non-communicative and therefore permanent form, and it is this that separates the spirit/soul being off from the realm of spirituality. At the same time it is the forming of resistance (chapter 7) that enables knowing to come about. The first occurrence of ego-consciousness is sparked off by this creating of forms, a substitute until the consciousness soul or the spirit self is formed. This is why the dissolving of the non-communicative forms has to go hand in hand with the formation of the various kinds of ego-consciousness that are stage by stage becoming freer and freer of form (consciousness soul, spirit self etc.). In the concentration exercise both aims are being pursued.

Theme for contemplation:
19. Attentiveness is essential to any experience.

Theme for meditation:
19. Attentiveness seeks itself.

18.
The concentration exercise[41]

The attentiveness of an adult is seldom directed towards one single theme, and actually only then when the theme is very attractive or when duty calls. In the latter case problems can easily arise. In everyday life the attentiveness is like a ball of wool which ten cats have been playing with for hours. It is partly that life forces us to direct our attention to several objects at once. But we never experience them as such, that is, in themselves or empty, but only from the moment onwards when they have metamorphosed into an image of cognition. So it seems to us that we are surrounded by a world of objects without asking how they make their appearance or to whom. The fact that attentiveness is not experienced consciously in itself indicates that the source of it lies in the superconscious.

For the basic exercise let us choose a simple object we are familiar with (a button, needle, spoon, pencil, ring or suchlike) and look at it very carefully if necessary; then we put it aside or close our eyes and try to visualize the object. This will happen all the better the more we allow the picture to 'appear', like a memory. As though we were asking ourselves: What does the object look like? Experience shows that the object is very fleeting — other images, thoughts etc. soon appear — so we try to hold on to it by talking to it: 'Stay a little while', 'Don't be in a hurry', but we could say anything else we like, and even send it away: 'Go away if you want to!' — as long as we *talk to it* the image will stay. Words (in our thinking) are of course only necessary at the beginning, later on we can 'talk to it' by means of a visualized exclamation ('Hum, heh') and still later simply by focusing our inner attention on it. The focus is different according to whether one is simply seeing something or whether one is addressing it. The holding of the image is then being done with a relaxed, gentle will.

By holding the image and by imagining the object functioning (e.g. the spoon spooning), the intensity of the attentiveness grows. This leads to an important turning point in experiencing it—namely that we identify with the functioning object or with the idea of it. To put it differently, we experience the understanding of the object consciously and continuingly—in everyday life understanding is also an identifying of the (thinking) attentiveness with what we understand, only this experience is homeopathically short (like presence of mind) and therefore does not become conscious. We can have similar experiences of identification in the theatre or when listening to music: In both cases what is experienced does not remain an object. The attentiveness can increase to an unlimited extent and it can, immediately after the experience of identification, still experience itself in its independence. This experience is called the 'I-am experience', and it is the forming of the first true I, of the spirit self, and consciousness of self. If this experience occurs in the form of a flashing up it is called the consciousness soul, if it acquires permanence it is called spirit self.[42]

An outcome of this exercise, which is no less important, can consist in the attentiveness being aimed in one particular direction so that there is a direct flow from its origin to the theme. This brings order into the life of thinking, feeling and will, whereas without such an exercise this is in most cases chaotic. A person becomes concentrated within himself, becomes increasingly a shaper of his soul life, which also has to do with the I-experience of course.

The stronger the stream of attentiveness becomes the

more the I can experience itself as formfree, i.e. the closer it comes to its superconscious source, and coming closer to this source means — together with the I-experience — the possibility of spiritual experiences. For the superconscious part of a human being as the source of attentiveness has access to the spiritual world where a person's soul/spiritual being dwelt before birth. The superconscious (the 'higher members') is that part of the soul/spiritual being which does not join up with the inherited organism. By means of concentration the I-consciousness can lift itself into the sphere of the superconscious.

The attentiveness, as it becomes more and more form-free, is capable of experiencing the quality of the attentiveness of children and grown-ups, i.e. is capable of grasping an individuality and the possible ways in which it can actually transform itself. At the same time it also gives it the ability to be able to improvise the necessary pedagogical steps. This is possible because the one carrying out the exercise is going in an ego-conscious manner through the experiences which the baby — without I-consciousness and still in an undivided consciousness — has passed through until the coming of its egoity. This way of experiencing things stretches from the undivided consciousness, which we have no means of describing, through the stage of experiencing the world as will, feeling and becoming, which continually interchange with one another, as far as the experiencing of the world of objects in their duality. This arises simultaneously with the feeling of self. This and the egoity are the starting point for the one doing the exercises. The I-am experience begins directly after he has achieved identity with the theme. If the attentiveness is strong enough it becomes clear to us that all conscious experiences — also the image of the chosen object — are metamorphoses of our attentiveness, and because attentiveness is the 'substance' of our true I,[43] the experience of identifying can arise.[44] After this turning point the attentiveness begins to experience itself as such, and in the course of this experience it moves backwards along its path to its source. The healing forces arising from this exercise are many, but primarily it brings order into the soul. This is experienced as tranquility.

Theme for contemplation:
20. Attentiveness, thinking, feeling, willing, memory etc. are gifts.

Theme for meditation:
20. Concentration leads to its own source.

19.
The inner attitude

If we have understood the content of the first seven chapters (phenomenology) of this book and by applying our minds have drawn our conclusions as to how to behave to the small child, that is a sign of goodwill, though as far as education goes we shall not be able, practically, to change much. For we know full well that people's soul/spiritual being is hardly altered by reasoned arguments and that what *really* matters for the child is the attitude of a person's whole heart and soul. It is preferable, of course, if we restrain ourselves from venting an outburst of rage rather than giving way to it; but rage in an adult's soul, whether it is expressed or not, is at least real to the child, meaning that it has an effect on it. We all know what a difficult achievement it is to hold back all trace of rage. And this is just what we would want for the child.

Our intellect has the task of understanding the results of research. But by doing this we do not change very much; we do, however, recognize at least the direction for self-education. Changes in our being occur usually through experience. Simple perceptions and thoughts cannot take the place of experiences. If a piece of knowledge acquires the status of experience, possibly repeatedly, this can totally change us. Knowledge becomes experience by not remaining merely thought but by taking effect in living thinking that is wordless, above the level of speech, in perceptive feeling and willing, i.e. becoming real. A piece of knowledge becomes experience when the attentiveness that thinks or feels or wills it experiences it at the same time in action.

After the mind has grasped a topic, then contemplation (deep, concentrated thinking) of what has been grasped, and the subsequent meditation[45] on what has passed through contemplation, leads into the part of soul life where it becomes experience. The contemplations and meditations in the text serve in this way. Meditation is simply deep concentration on the theme, on an idea.

We could also call the newly awakened capacity for improvisation 'empathy'. If we *feel* what is going on in a child we usually also seize on to what needs doing. We can call this capacity meditative seeing. Good, 'born' kindergarten teachers acquire this in a few years of training for their profession. Others can acquire it through exercises.

Let us summarize what the phenomenology of a child tells us.

Similar to an adult, a child is a spiritual being who makes use of a body in order to cope with the earthly world. As the spiritual part of our being is not visible to the senses we usually see the child, and adults as well, as bodies that are the bearers of certain memories, habits, thoughts, feelings and expressions of will. Once we have experienced our spiritual ego as a self-aware soul or spirit self, then we know in our whole being that all human beings, even babies, have this being in them potentially. That is, our view of people, including children, changes. We look at sense perception like someone who can read a text. Those who cannot read see merely the sense perceptible part of the text. When they learn to read their perception changes. At the least they know that what they see has a meaning, and that this meaning has produced the visible part.

So we acquire respect for people, and for children too. With this attitude we shall keep on discovering phenomena in children that arise not out of their bodily nature but from their spiritual being. These are primarily the non-inherited, specifically human abilities and their signs (see chapter 4). We shall also listen attentively and not dismiss it as products of fantasy if a child speaks sometimes of the spiritual experiences it still has.

Just as in the case of man-made objects, the meaning (function) has to be there before the implementing of the object (similar to communicating, when what appears by way of the signs has to precede the signs), we can also consider things not made by human beings in the same way, namely as signs which we cannot read at first. Everything we perceive in nature through our senses is a sign. This is what the sense world looks like to a baby. We can experience this by doing the meditation on perceiving.[46] The sense world consists of signs conveying meaning. Nature is creative will that has been halted and held fast, and it rays out feeling and meaning. It is not difficult to experience this raying-out feeling, even if at first we do not understand it. This experience is important because it transforms our relationship to nature without sentimentality, and ultimately without rationality determined by self-interest. (What will happen to humankind when the natural resources run out?) And in this way we come a step closer to how a small child experiences things.

Once we have grasped that in a world where physical matter does not exist there can be only direct, immediate communication (no signs), then we at least have an inkling that in that world existence consists of this kind of communication, and that a child comes from this world into ours as a spiritual/soul being. It acquires an inherited body, and its task and also the task of the environment helping it is to form a connection of the spirit/soul to this body. The body is taken hold of by the spirit through the gestures of expression, above all by speaking, for the body is by its very nature the sign part of the person, whereas the spirit/soul is the meaning part which imparts through the body its changing meanings. The observation has been made that children who do not learn to speak (this does not have to be verbal but also includes passive listening), that is, where there is no dialogue with the environment, the children do not take hold of their body properly either. The help a child can receive in this respect from the adult environment is the initiative to communicate and people speaking to the child. This 'speaking' does not have to be audible to start with — until about the fourth or fifth month — but it ought to happen with total dedication, as also the conversations later on. You should speak in simple words, but not by any means 'baby language', nor constantly speak sweet nothings. You can happily leave it on its own a lot so that it has the chance to digest what it has heard. Just wait until the baby itself takes up the thread again.

It should be a fundamental part of a teacher's attitude[47] to endeavour to have a feeling of wonder regarding phenomena one would otherwise take for granted. A feeling of wonder comes naturally to a small child, because in order to have it, it does not have to fight against what hinders adults from having it: that they cover up every phenomenon by 'showering' it with readymade concepts. The exercise of openmindedness[48] can help us to hold back with concepts so that we meet the phenomenon as though for the first time. Although it is only a substitute for direct communication which was inevitably lost (and of which adults are quite incapable), yet speaking, being able to communicate through signs, appears to be for a baby a joy and wonder — for it is eager to experience this over and over again. When we think about it, it really is a wonder that even as adults we can sometimes understand ourselves.

The principle of self-development is that we endeavour to create in ourselves consciously the kind of experience a baby has. If we cannot achieve this it is helpful to know of this way of experiencing, although it usually has no effect when dealing with a child. It is the same with the baby's fundamental impulses to do good. Unless adults discover this in themselves — without just imagining it in a sentimental way — they will hardly notice this impulse in babies. We ought to have the unshakable conviction that human beings are originally orientated towards the Good and that egoity only arrives later — as a necessary intermediate stage in evolution. If it were not to arise it would be a type of handicap.

The need for self-education in adults and the direction it should go in is founded in the impressionability of a baby, which is usually seen as 'imitation'. The child is formed and shaped more or less — in individually different ways — by what we *are*. What we say and think about ourselves, our illusions in this respect, are as good as non-existent for the child.

With regard to star children there arises for example the problem of the 'respect' they expect from us. This must be *genuine*; by putting on a pretence all we achieve is that these children sense that we are liars. The question can be put this way: Do we have respect for ourselves? — Surely only when we experience ourselves as spiritual beings, otherwise we would have little reason to respect ourselves. If we did go through this experience we would see in everyone, children included, a being deserving of our respect.

From what has been said it should have become clear how important it is to talk to the child even at the stage of passively acquiring speech, when it only understands but does not yet speak actively itself. In this period the whole attentiveness of the child is receptive and, as it does not itself speak as yet, its attention is undivided. Whilst speaking to a baby we should give our whole attention to the child. Otherwise the inner reality behind the acoustic signs will only be there in a fragmentary way, and it is just this inner reality which gives the child the experience of the meaning of the spoken words. If, while the adult is telling the child something, in addition to the actual message his consciousness is preoccupied with the day's worries, problems and fears, the child cannot tell which part of the contents belong to the acoustic signs: the result will be unclear, confused thinking. It is also obvious that by means of a radio or some other medium that does not convey the presence of an actual live consciousness the child will merely learn to speak 'parrot-fashion'; whilst if adults only give partial attention to a child at the stage when it is learning to speak, this in all probability leads to speech and behavioural problems. It is obviously better to concentrate on what you are saying when you talk to a child.

The mother tongue gives the child not only word concepts but also grammar which contains (together with a vocabulary) a specific way of thinking, its style and a system of thought. As the child is born with an attunement to meaning it is able to speak correct grammar without knowing the rules, the grammatical concepts, consciously. In fact adults speak a language well, even a foreign language, when they have reached the point where they have 'forgotten' the rules. A language is an organic unity or whole. A child absorbs it superconsciously and with its feeling (this is why a multi-lingual child does not confuse the words, phonetics and grammar of the various languages). It is important that the adults in the child's environment, as well as giving it their full attention, bring the mother tongue to the child properly pronounced, and in a pure, undistorted form.

Theme for contemplation:
21. What is an adult's most important task when educating a small child?

Theme for meditation:
21. Light is formfree.

20.
Developing the senses, acquiring speech, forming concepts

The differentiation of the individual areas of the senses from out of the archetypal sense is a stage of development in our acquiring of concepts, for we perceive largely in a 'conceptual' way, i.e. we perceive the reason why we have a conceptual realm, or it dawns on us in the process of perception.[49] The expression 'conceptual realm' is used instead of 'concept' because whereas 'concept' designates the forms arising in thinking, the conceptual realm covers not only these but also those forms and structures grasped by feeling and by the reversed will. In the case of the child structures arise first of all in the feeling and will. This can happen best if the people in the adult environment endeavour to experience the words, the concepts. Usually we do not experience the words in our feeling and will. For a child to be able to understand a word it hears it must experience its meaning. People who speak to it can help it do this by holding in their consciousness, while speaking, the pictorial image of the word, if it has one. For images are formed by the feeling, the feeling will. The word must not be divided into its various sounds but imagined as a picture. Words that are not signs for something sense perceptible, like for instance adverbs, can also be felt in their inner gesture, and all the more easily the more concentration one brings to thinking them while one speaks. The inner gesture of – for instance – 'but', 'or', 'although', is not describable but is nevertheless feelable, and if the speaker feels this it helps the child to a feeling understanding. You can practise feeling the inner gesture by comparing, with concentration, the various gestures of words of this kind, without describing this in words, as their very meaning replaces the impossibility of describing them. You can do the same thing with other kinds of words, adjectives (deep, red, heavy) and nouns (feeling, pain, diligence), etc. Mark you, it is not a matter of the sounds or the sound structure but of the meaning, from which the word gets its shade of feeling. You must not forget that what the child first gets hold of in the words is their archetypal meaning, which enables them to be applied in very different circumstances (e.g. the *end* of the way, of the day, of a friendship, or of someone's efforts).

Obviously the development of the senses rests on a rich world of perception. As the differentiation of the archetypal sense begins in the feeling and will it is fitting to bring the child in touch with a world of perception that is rich in feeling, i.e. with natural objects, natural materials and things made out of them, as we have no concepts for nature but only concept-replacing names, so that a feeling relationship is not disturbed by the element of thought.

Regarding acquiring speech, in addition to what has already been mentioned a further feature of speaking to the child should be stressed, namely honesty. Adults should speak with *honesty* (a demand which ought actually to apply to any form of speaking), and only say what they really mean. If they don't, there will be severe consequences for the child. If, while they are speaking, something different is going on in their thinking, feeling and will the child will get 'confused', for it picks up everything living in the speaker's soul life. Just as in the spiritual world there is no pretence or misunderstanding, we are transparent to the child, often long after the appearing of egoity.

Adults could formulate the general task of education in

the following negative way: I must protect the child from myself.

Since a baby does not obtain its first concepts through sense perception, as the naïve kind of child psychology assumes (according to the same pattern as its false picture of the way adults form concepts) but on the contrary obtains them through direct signless communication, adults should, when relating to the realm of concepts, make sure that their minds are governed by clarity and a healthy attitude. They should be quite clear in their minds about what they understand, and what is merely a more or less inscrutable shell of a word. In everyday life we make use of a great number of words whose meaning we do not fully understand. As the child receives its first concepts from us our lack of clarity is transferred to the child. These half-concepts, because of the way we hold on to them in an emotional, egoistic manner, are very tenacious, and take the place of understanding. This is one of the sources of confused thinking both in the child and in adults. So it would be fitting from time to time to undertake a revision of our judgements and concepts, the words we use and our habits.

The clarity or transparency of our concepts is particularly important for star children because long after they have begun to speak in the first person they notice the inner uncertainty arising in the speaker when he uses words behind which there is no complete understanding.

Theme for contemplation:
22. Let us look for the feeling that will indicate which of our 'concepts' are unclear.

Theme for meditation:
22. In understanding all is light.

21.
The feeling of self

The development of the feeling of self is an occurrence with a double face. It divides the consciousness from its sources, making the person more or less independent of the impulses coming from the spiritual world and therefore creating the basis of his subsequent freedom, of his true ego-consciousness, of his true I.[50] In order that feeling of self can arise, sentient forces from out of the sentient body have first to become free and then mould themselves into a secondary 'body', into a form. The sentient body is a form that receives perceptions and reacts to them. It regulates the biological processes according to the state of soul life. If the person feels endangered then, by way of a regular process that is not conscious, there is a change in blood pressure, pulse, the chemical composition of the blood and the brain, the breath, etc. Through the influence of the (not self-aware) spirit/soul, right from birth onward, forces become free from every part of the body which, in the first place, become forces of knowing or of attentiveness or (in other words) of love. Under the influence of the egoistic environment they partly take on the mould of the new form, and this process is speeded up and strengthened if these freed forces are not used. The release of forces can be understood from the well-known example of the change of teeth around the seventh year. The life forces which bring forth the second teeth thereafter become free and can be used as forces of intelligence for learning. This is why the change of teeth is a sign of being ready to go to school.

It is important to follow up and bring influence to bear on this process, for as this new sentient form — it can be called the ego body—this form of the feeling of self develops, it impairs the access to spirituality and direct communication. If by this time the child has not yet sufficiently internalized its mother tongue, this will become more and more difficult later on. The development of thinking will also be influenced for, at the beginning, thinking is inspired, meaning that it is accompanied by perceptive feeling (which later on is confined to the feeling for the rightness of things). The more the child, between the ages of one and three, meets with things of an abstract, technical, rational nature, the earlier and more intensely does the child's thinking separate off from perceptive feeling. The child's feeling loses its perceptive character because of this, and the impulse to have a feeling of self is strengthened. Its thinking becomes colder, more rational, less intuitive.[51] Contact with older siblings and children in whom the egoity has already developed hastens the development of this in the smaller child, and this is why second children usually mature faster than the firstborn ones.

Adults can influence these changes, especially by way of their own soul structure, i.e. according to how far their own life is governed by egoity. In other words: to what extent they are loving people. Apart from this fundamental influence the release of the forces of feeling can be promoted by an involvement with pictures that are as artistic as possible (picture books) and by the telling of fairytales in a healthy way, as fairytales actually are a series of pictures which have to be imagined, otherwise the fairytale will not come across. Fairytales also connect perceptive feeling with thinking. You should choose from fairytales (not didactic ones), ones that have proved themselves over generations.

Good story tellers experience the fairytale pictures in

their feelings. This can be acquired by meditating on the pictures[52] so that a perceptive feeling for them is called to life. Any kind of 'interpreting' of the stories by means of a theory or world outlook works against this capacity.

When teachers know what is going on in the child through the arising of egoity, they will judge accordingly the 'stage of defiance' that accompanies it, and be able to deal with it.

Because a star child's sheath of the feeling of self is thin, that is, less developed than in 'normal' children, fewer of the released forces are drawn into it and a large surplus remains freely available. This is evident in the tremendous energy star children have, and which needs to be engaged. A great many of these children grow very early beyond the age of fairytales, partly because they experience spirituality more immediately and intensely, in fact they still to a certain extent live in it; and partly because they need to become involved in earthly matters at an earlier age — they are after all mature souls. Some, at least, of these star children are interested early on in science and technology. Many of them learn to read, write and do arithmetic independently, a long time before they go to school. The so-called 'Waldorf principles' can only be applied on a very reduced scale; there have been cases where they have made these children more difficult. Observant kindergarten teachers have already noticed this.

Theme for contemplation:
23. Why is it not desirable that a person has too strong an egoity?

Theme for meditation:
23. It is only light that can perceive light.

22.
The religiousness of a small child and its cultivation
by Annie Kühlewind

From what has been presented in chapter 13 it follows that adults would do well to avoid as much as possible interfering artificially in the 'religious' life of a child. Adults should not initiate anything that is contrary to what comes from the child itself, nor try to impose adult religious ideas on the child's consciousness. If they did they would steer religious feelings in the direction of intellectuality, which would soon kill them off. If the child asks questions with regard to religion we should give our answers in the awareness that for the child the whole world, every single thing, even its own body, is an object of the feeling of unity and gratitude, from out of which later on love will blossom.

The far-reaching, steady gaze of the small child is a sign of a kind of attentiveness which is uninfluenced, free of egoity, and open to its surroundings. There is no question yet of it having faith or trust. The child does not have faith and does not have trust in 'somebody'. Its awareness of life is still not separate from the living awareness in other people, there is no gap between these, therefore nothing to bridge because there is no feeling of separateness. It would actually be a bridging gesture if the child were to have faith or belief in what another person says. It is not a question of the child accepting with inner affirmation the opinion of adults. All these positive gestures appear only after the openness, which is not conscious, has ceased, and a part of the attentiveness which is free and can identify itself with other things has already united with the feeling of the body and the child's consciousness look out at the world from this dualistic position.

Prayer was born out of the consciousness of dualism — according to the apocryphal gospels Abraham was the first person to pray. Before him human beings obviously lived in a relationship of inner dialogue with the Godhead. Prayer is a plea for the restoration of the lost unity, and it arises out of being separated.

With few exceptions adults approach the idea of God through mental images, not intuitions. This idea, as it is not experienced, is abstract and remote. To their feeling consciousness the soul gestures in the realm of faith are not absolutely real. Their faith needs props. If they are not capable of recapturing, through conscious inner work, the lost attentiveness of their early childhood, they usually seek help in the rules and techniques of the confessional, and get caught up in them and remain stuck. Then the focus of their prayer turns from the will to the restoration of identity, and prayer becomes more egoistic. The rules and regulations rob their consciousness of the chance to question and search, and restrict its scope. They then get answers to questions they have not asked.

What can adults do to prolong the period in which the innate kind of consciousness of the small child can continue to develop? They should foster all the things that nourish the child's capacity for wonder and devotion. This can be done by slowing down as it were the flow of life round the child. Allow the child to get absorbed in wonder, do not explain things to it in advance, and do not ask it questions in return. Least of all should thoughts concerning the supersensible realm which have not been experienced be put into words, such as God, heaven, angels, etc. — or very seldom at most. For no thought can convey a corresponding truth about this realm. You have to wait until the innate capacities and the slowly developing duality meet—then the questions about 'the other world' come of themselves. This seldom happens before the ninth year.

In his book *And There Was Light*, Jacques Lusseyran writes:[53]

My parents were heaven. I didn't say this to myself so precisely, and they never said it to me, but it was obvious. I knew very early, I am quite sure of it, that through them another Being concerned himself with me and even addressed himself to me. This Other I did not even call God. My parents spoke to me about God, but only later. I had no name for Him. He was just there and it was better so. Behind my parents there was someone, and my father and mother were simply the people responsible for passing along the gift. My religion began like this, which I think explains why I have never known doubt. This confession may be something of a surprise, but I set store by it because it will make so many other things clear, my recklessness, for instance.

I was always running; the whole of my childhood was spent running. Only I was not running to catch hold of something. That is a notion for grown-ups and not the notion of a child. I was running to meet everything that was visible, and everything that I could not yet see. I travelled from assurance to assurance, as though I were running a race in relays.

A child experiences soul/spiritual presence behind everyone and everything, and it has the experience that all these presences are shone upon by a further mightier presence. It experiences the world of the superconscious in a more intense and true way than the adult does, because for the child it is not transcendental. The child lives in it neither with thought nor with everyday feelings. While adults give their faith content and form and approach the beings that work in the superconscious, intuitive world with their *thinking*, the child's soul/spiritual being is at home in that landscape. Its far-reaching attentiveness goes directly to the realm where nothing is divided.

This undivided state of being is not a 'something' that is outside consciousness. The soul/spiritual being of the child is of the same quality as its source and creator. It is from out of an identity with this that our earthly intelligence grows.

Faculties directed towards earthly matters can develop healthily if their object is not thrust on the child. Children learn by themselves to do arithmetic and to read or write, and they do this all the better the less they are told or forced to do so. And it is the same with other capacities necessary in life. There is invariably a danger of having skills and knowledge forced on a child when the child's environment is uniformly intellectual.

With adults the shadow of their superconscious life appears in the form of thoughts. Their not-conscious association with the divine/spiritual world manifests as a shadow formation in the form of religious precepts.

The life of a small child's consciousness knows no such shadows. It has a direct connection to superconscious life, its sources and creator-forces, uncluttered by thoughts about it, like a kind of dim memory. Adults cannot pass on to a child any religious precepts because they lack a knowledge of the child's immediate situation.

The adult could learn from the child of a far-reaching, independent attentiveness, of faith and trust in a world that is not dualistic, a world where there are not two kinds of existence, one that is spiritual and one that is earthly.

Both of these have been nurtured at the same source and are therefore in harmony with one another, if this harmony could be consciously brought to realization and made the aim of the future.

By means of perceptive feeling adults can bring themselves to see, through inner work, that they can impart earthly intelligence in a proper way to the child if they themselves get in touch with the source of this intelligence, which is identical with the source of the superconscious being of the child and of every human being. If the child's parents do not at least sometimes achieve this undivided consciousness, the child will hardly be able to have the experience that through them, its parents, the light of their own spiritual homeland is shining. The way to the earthly homeland is prepared and strengthened through the presence of the spiritual one.

When adults speak the word 'God', and 'God' is said with intention, they do not need to give any explanation — the child will feel and understand who it is. If there is no intuitive experience behind the word, this will add to the lack of clarity in earthly consciousness. Every proof, every explanation damages the sense for truth. The idea of God should find its place in the child's still far-reaching, formfree attentiveness, but being taught about it and hearing frequent mention of the name of God will prevent this happening. A comprehensive, far-reaching concept should arise, such as Jacques Lusseyran describes: 'I had no name for Him. He was just there, and it was better so... My parents spoke to me about God, but only later...' When this idea becomes part of the far-reaching attentiveness of the child, it acquires a place in the holiness which, to the child, streams to it from its environment, because with its whole soul life it lives in the meanings of things and people, not in sense perceptible phenomena.

Intense attentiveness is directed to this sphere precisely because here the abilities in the direction of perception reverberate together with, become identical with, the meanings living in the phenomena.

When a child attends a festival, the point is not what the child thinks of as being the content of it; the important things are the joy attached to it and the experience of beauty. Joy is the medium in which the superconscious world appears in human beings. Words of joy are: 'I can reach higher'; 'There are greater things than I'; 'I am the world'; 'Love is flowing'; 'I am a gift'; 'We exist for ever'. And because joy is the most important thing, the emphasis is in joining together at a level above that of ordinary life, within a framework of beauty, and pervaded by an awareness of it being a special occasion. If joy is being experienced then a gift can be a suitable addition to the festival.

To keep the attentiveness uncluttered and fully focused the content of the festival should not be explained in terms of the adults' store of concepts. If possible, you should make up a fairytale yourself that has to do with the nuance of feeling and feeling content of the festival. By doing this we give the child a chance to move freely towards the meaning which the festival reveals to the people on earth. The fairytale should also not hinder an understanding of the festival being able to grow from year to year.

Examples:

At Christmas you can give a simple account of the story of the shepherds and the wise men, the events in Bethlehem (with songs).

At Easter the Tibetan folk-tale of the hare that was prepared to sacrifice itself for the little old man in the Moon. Seeds are sown in the earth, new life arises.[54]

At Whitsun: How did great grief turn to great joy? How

did the mighty wind come to appear in the house? The language of the apostles, whom everyone understood (with song, dance and play).

At Christmas you can have the Christ Child bringing the present to start with, but around the seventh year (even earlier with some children) this ought to change. 'Has the Christ Child been to you, and did he whisper in your ear what would bring your Grannie joy?' Then the Christ Child enters the heart and gives advice about our fellow human beings.

A prayer in the evening is possible — all that can be shared by accompanying adults in real devotion, and this depends on the extent to which they can concentrate and shut everything else out of their consciousness. No observances have to be 'adhered to', no ideas or advice from other people. It will only be convincing for children if it comes from the heart of those close to them.

The evening prayer can be said kneeling and with the hands together. You will notice when the time comes for giving up this form and the child wants to be left alone to pray. Maybe it wants to pray with you for a long time, or maybe not. When it prays by itself you should not enquire whether it has done so.

Before mealtimes a short grace can be said. It is a matter of sensing the moment when praying aloud has to stop so that the child can attain inner speech, a wordless thinking-feeling. If this moment is missed (the moment is about the age of seven or eight) then boredom arises, it is said mechanically, and it becomes trivial.

You can talk about anything that you yourself *feel* about. So it is possible to talk about guardian angels, angels altogether, the homeland of the dead etc. if it is relevant.

Before the child wakes up to thinking about its own body praying aloud should change into silent prayer. The child will become conscious that the physical body excludes every other physical presence. The egoity, the feeling of self increases, the world becomes more and more dualistic, because the soul that is becoming more personal and the spirit that is active in the superconscious realm become detached from one another. The superconscious source of our perception and thinking is now no longer felt, and the one who perceives and thinks is left on his own.

The place where, earlier on, a radiation was discernable behind everything, is now taken up by illusions accompanied by rampant feelings. These are not to be avoided for they belong constitutionally to human life. At the same time all earthly misery and suffering comes from this.

After the childlike oneness of soul and spirit has ceased, thinking and feeling have to fluctuate from one side to the other in an empty space. This space provides the hope that the soul can be united again with the superconscious source and its creator. Through increasing objective attentiveness and high quality (real) artistic education, interest or curiosity can be aroused for the subject of the attentiveness, for the one who does the looking, the seeing and the doing. The more intense the attentiveness becomes the greater grows the surrounding sphere with which the spiritual/soul element can connect, until it acquires a feeling for the very core that can restore unity with everything. This inner activity is in harmony with the orientation towards the Good (chapter 3), is supported by it and appears in the form of creative, outgoing activity. Without any outer directions, ties or restrictions, or any negotiating, the creative loving nature of the child will become active in what is from now on a conscious awakening and resurrection of its childlike spirituality.

There is something comical about it when adults want to teach children, especially star children, about religiousness. In this domain most children are much more at home than the adults who try to do the teaching. If, in addition, the instructing is given without there being any basis in experience, then, in star children in particular, an intense antipathy is aroused towards religious thought sequences of any kind.

Theme for contemplation:

24. What are the differences between the consciousness of a small child and adults? What does this lead to regarding the way the latter behave?

Theme for meditation:

24. Feeling is a more powerful reality than thinking.

23.
Children, star children and adults

Small children 'imitate'. People should understand this thoroughly and take it deeply to heart; then it will point a way that adults can take in their constant work on themselves, a way to a steady transformation. Children 'imitate' what we *are* not what we think we are or would like to be, and they are formed purely by what we are. Fortunately this is done with individual selectiveness. And this is more marked in the case of star children than 'normal' ones. But adults would do well to be deeply convinced that *every* child comes into this world with a general orientation to do the Good, and in addition, with a totally individual mission. The difference between 'normal' children and star children is solely that with regard to both these impulses the latter are more conscious, more self-aware.

We must not understand the term 'star children' in any sense as a new category or as a typological stamp, for in reality we find a continuous spectrum of children without there being any sharp dividing line. Star children exist just as darkness and light exist without our being able to specify a sharp boundary between them.

In keeping with this, the proper attitude to star children is to use a more 'improved' edition of the recommendations for treating children than apply for 'normal' children. 'Improved' means in this case adhering to these in a stricter and less compromising manner. What can be 'adhered to' are rough and very general rules, things any good teacher would include as a matter of course. The actual task consists in individualizing these general 'rules' to suit the individual child and the adults themselves. This is the difficult, very demanding part of it and—as children develop—makes constant work for the adults. If they are attentive they will get a lot of help from the child, especially star children. As they demand greater transformation in the adult, we shall take them as our models. What is described here regarding them is the best thing for any child's education.

Children are human beings, individuals, and come to earth with very considerable capacities which adults have lost. There is no reason to look down on them and feel superior to them. We are confronting a whole person, to whom we owe *respect*. It is worth looking back each evening at the way we have treated the child during the day. The main aspects are respect and honesty. Dishonesty makes no sense: children see through us, feel into us. Respect means not forcing anything on the children, any habit or standard practice, without explaining it or—if it is something more general—having their consent. They will consent to anything that is right, once it is understood. If the children are still too small for this, we should 'discuss' it with them all the same, unilaterally, in which case they will certainly feel your good intention. If the child can already speak it should be allowed to take an active part in any decisions that concern it. We can let the children themselves make suggestions with regard to discipline, hygiene, habits and the agenda for the day. Always give them the chance to *choose*, and if at all feasible don't tell them to do something without giving them the possibility of choice. The reason should always be explained.

The child should be a partner in his education, not an object. It should if at all possible be given no negative 'orders', no prohibitions; these can always be transformed into positive suggestions. Instead of 'don't do that' it is preferable to say 'it would be better to do this'. Let us give the child the chance to *grow*—we can seldom know in advance what it really wants to be. Ask the child to help us. If for instance it wants to do something with us for which our presence is necessary, yet we have no time, then describe the situation to it and ask it: What shall I do about it?

We have to set limits to the children's activities; but they themselves should set these boundaries or help us to do so. Star children need a great deal of space for their bubbling energy—let *them* plan and limit this space.

It is highly recommended to watch the way these children play, do their jobs, eat, drink, clean their teeth, etc.; their thoroughness, their movements, whether they are skillful or clumsy. If we are intuitive enough the necessary ideas will occur to us while we are watching or when we think or meditate about it afterwards. Watch them especially when they are together with other children, or when they are in the company of star children. If they become rebellious, arrogant, aggressive, this is a sign that they need new, more demanding tasks. It is particularly important to notice this in a class setting; the teacher can save himself a lot of trouble if he constantly gives the star children tasks which stretch them to their limit. New tasks, new limits— every child *wants* precise, not confused limits. Indulgence on the part of parents or teachers is of course the worst of choices. The adult should never place the child in a category, for firstly this hinders the child from changing, secondly you will nowadays hardly find typological classification of any value, and thirdly, if the child is sensitive to the classification he will either bring it to realization or go all out to disprove it.

The best way to go about things in school is to decide on the regulations, the arranging of the day and general conduct, in fact everything belonging to the life of the class, together with the children right from the beginning (class 1 in fact), avoiding if possible the forbidding of anything. If the positive side is fully described and the children have understood it and accepted it, then hardly a single child will do anything that would need forbidding.

That teachers can achieve anything merely on the strength of the authority inherent in their position as teacher, is an illusion today. What has an effect is solely what they are as human beings. If the teacher has achieved inner discipline through consciousness training, problems with discipline are far more easily solved than any other way. If the teachers are concentrated then the children in their class will be concentrated – (possibly with exceptions). If they are not concentrated themselves, why should the children be?

With regard to star children we can assume, for our inner orientation, that they are older than we are – we often even have this feeling consciously; it will be our surest guide, or at least protect us from disparaging them, or thinking of them in that way. The most difficult thing for parents and teachers to do is to meet a star child who has already been 'spoilt' and has become 'difficult', and treat him in such a way that the damage can be healed. In this case too, we can reckon on the 'difficult' child perceiving – in *his* way – our understanding and good intention, without our putting it into words. The best, most important 'communication' always happens – even between adults – without words or signs.

This is why I will now hold my tongue.

Theme for contemplation:
25. How can one be honest with oneself?

Theme for meditation:

25. In the superconscious we are bound together know-
    ingly.

24.
Afterword and consolation

The author has the hope that there will be some readers who will have an understanding of the following: namely the fact that these new children, star children, are coming into the world with the mission to change our lives for the better; but that they can only succeed in this if adults do not hinder them from doing so through the education they grant them. To prevent this happening adults have to muster sufficient insight and courage, and do the necessary inner work.

Even with the best of goodwill and conviction, and if we take all the suggestions made in this book seriously and try hard to put them into practice, there is no avoiding mistakes. But this ought not to deprive anyone of their courage and bring them to despair. For all children are capable of feeling, beneath the surface, the true impulse behind our mistakes and misunderstandings: they will have understanding for our stumbling and forgive us. If we do our utmost the children will come to meet us with their sensitivity, and we are not aspiring to be perfect teachers. This is why thoroughly honest intentions, and a radically understanding attitude, are so important.

APPENDIX I
The ending of childhood
by Annie Kühlewind

If we adults endeavour to understand what is going on in a child at the threshold to puberty then our relationship can take on a communicative character, even if our conversation does not directly touch on the crises a nine to twelve-year old has to struggle through. It is neither knowledge nor expectations that bring about this character of communication but attentiveness which will enable us to visualize a kind of unfolding. This is the right kind of help for the child in its development, as it promotes the inner connection between the adult and the child. This kind of connection is a support in situations where direct help is inappropriate.

We adults living in the environment of the child must expend all our forces in order to understand what is going on. This expenditure of forces has the same spiritual quality as the development going on in the child. It is the quality of human development. The effort to understand is a mutual connecting link between the soul forces of both parties. By continuously offering an attitude of understanding we adults can prepare the space a child needs to unfold its entitlement to 'becoming grown-up'. Adults should accompany with inner and outer movements the inner and outer movements of the child — ones which indicate a 'letting go' of childhood. The inner movements spur us on to have the right thoughts, arouse in us the right words, and inspire our deeds. What kind of movements are these?

Rejoice over the fact that human life is ruled by reason

that can lead to this changing and evolving, and that this force of reason is active in the children. We have to observe this attentively and assist their individual development. Neither indulgence nor the desire to have everything remain as it is must be allowed to play a leading role. We must take notice of the fact that new things are awakening in the being of the child. It is advisable to recognize the genuine cause of a negative phenomenon — and there are often all too many of these at this age — and to cultivate what can grow from it. For instance we should not respond to stubbornness with an even greater stubbornness but confront the child's will with tasks that are more demanding than any previous ones. It is good to give children the chance to develop their own initiative. It is even better if the adults' attentiveness is sensitive enough to read from the kind of defiance being offered what is needed at that particular moment in order to keep communication open. We shall refrain from describing the various solutions which have arisen in this field, as they do not lend themselves to generalization. Each individual will have to school their own attentiveness to understand the child in question, so that a suitable solution can be found.

The symptoms arising along the path of the child's development and the phases of the growing-up process are often misleading. The former charming, childlike picture of the child's soul/spiritual nature becomes distorted, chaotic. At this point adults face a difficult task. We can only shed light on the jungle of events by applying clear and loving attentiveness. The soul/spiritual aspect of the child's development does not become apparent with the same evident rapidity as the bodily aspect but is more hidden, individual and complicated. We cannot spare the child this, yet it is foreseeable that the crises occurring at this age will no longer be there when they have grown up.

Parents and teachers will find it easier to encounter these crises if they consider the child's life as a whole. This attitude allows space for liberated humour which can really help to overcome the problems of the beginning of the awkward age of adolescence, from nine to twelve, and the years that follow.

What is the child like before the ninth year, and what characterizes the fundamental difference compared with the period after the ninth year? What is the new factor that emerges between the ninth and the twelfth year?

Before school age, what helps a child find its way into the world, and triggers the budding thoughts and feelings is the sheer joy of perceiving the world. At this age children's perception is far deeper and richer than that of adults; it pulses through their whole being. It is the basis for their trust and for their all-encompassing thankfulness. Just to speak and to move makes them happy. There is no distance between the world and the ego of a child. The experience of an undivided world goes hand in hand with the joy of perceiving. If adults can observe thoroughly enough the way children make contact with the world then they are equipped to give children the kind of environment they need. If they try to increase, to 'beautify' the joy a child has in pure perception by giving it a 'beautiful doll' for instance — i.e. applying elements that correspond to the parents' outlook but not to the inner realities in the life of the child — this will damage the feelings of gratitide concealed within the joy of perception; the child's trust and faith, and even his or her imagination can suffer.

Up till roughly the ninth year feeling still goes hand in hand with bodily wellbeing, and can assist or retard development accordingly. Everybody responsible for the child carries a big responsibility in this area.

At the beginning of school age feeling is the bearer of

faith and devotion. When children hear fairytales they withdraw into the state of consciousness that belonged to their earlier years. We can observe clearly that while they are listening to fairytales their consciousness is far less sharp. They are dreamier than they are otherwise. At the same time they connect in feeling and will with the superconscious element of the fairytale, which is a mode of expression of a kind of intelligence which is the bearer of moral battles and values. The child will often hardly think any more about the story they have heard, yet it lives on in their feeling and will, and they will nevertheless be able to call it to memory and, when they do, they can reproduce it word for word. The biblical story of creation and other religious stories live on in children in a similar way, without making special demands on their thinking. They can be called to memory, but more as feeling memories than thought memories. The effect of this is a heartfelt, enthusiastic affirmation of life. By nourishing the children's attentiveness in this way we are strengthening their feeling-intelligence, which is very intense in the early years (kindergarten age). This kind of intelligence is in danger of getting lost if the child is given a strongly intellectual education. It will suffer damage if adults expose it to the pressures of learning at an early age, which are typical of our present civilization. In the process of learning, the feeling-intelligence is the basis for the intellect. It supports understanding because — according to the nature of a child's consciousness — feeling and thinking, in favourable conditions, do not separate from one another before the ninth year. If not learning intellectually, it is this feeling-intelligence which makes the child so gifted, receptive and so quick to learn.

What helps this feeling-intelligence unfold is the hearing of fairytales, legends and religious contents in fairytale form. Their affirmation of life and feeling-grasp of things cannot be compared with the religiousness of an adult, for children do not know that they 'have faith', that they are full of trust and reverence.

Faith and comfort, along with everything that a natural religious feeling can signify, are lost if religion appears as an accessory to knowledge. This is why adults should keep for children a style of approach in which they give them, by way of fairytales, legends, stories from the gospels and Christ legends, a clearly-felt, non-moralizing basis for security, not coupled with explanations and proofs. This will be of benefit and support their spontaneous devotion.

Security, and along with it the feeling for what is real, arise in connection with the superconscious. As long as this is strong then, for example, the validity of thinking will never be doubted. If the connection is weakened the feeling for reality begins to falter, and the person, the child, becomes unsure with regard to 'reality'.

If the sense of reality is sufficiently strengthened then the difficulties of the so-called 'pre-puberty-age' are more easily overcome. This will only be achieved if you have been doing the right thing with the child at the various stages of its earlier development, without having speeded up its progress. This is why the early years are so important.

Big changes begin to take place in the whole nature of children around their ninth year. This stage lasts until roughly the twelfth year. The experiences bound up with this pass over into children's behaviour, but a young person does not experience what is actually happening until after puberty, until around the sixteenth, seventeenth year. Nine-year-old children do not understand what is happening to them. They feel at the mercy of their development, and this produces anxiety, doubt and sadness. They have the impression they are all alone in the world, and they have the whole world against them. They long for the lost unity ('first love') even if they have a loving relationship with someone or something (e.g. a dog or a doll).

These feelings are the preconditions of a process of maturing through which the young person begins to feel capable of being able to reshape the world and assure himself of a part in it. He is now concerned with the question 'Who am I?' This process comes to a head around the sixteenth, seventeenth year.

In his autobiography *Theme and Variations* Bruno Walter describes a decisive experience when he was at the awkward age:

The growing boy, too, frequently manifested a strange condition of dreaminess, of absorption or enchantment, when all the wheels, usually turned so violently by the torrent of inward and outward phenomena, were halted and stood still as if they had been disconnected. I still recall how such a calm first manifested itself to me as a melancholy emotion, am still conscious of what I felt at the time, and can still visualize the place at which, a boy of ten or eleven, I experienced the spiritual thrill. I have forgotten how it came about that I was standing alone in the schoolyard—I may have been kept in as a punishment—but when I stepped out into the large square associated in my mind with the noise of playing or romping boys it seemed to me doubly empty and forsaken. I can see myself standing there, overwhelmed by the deep quiet. While I listened to it and the soft wind, I felt an unknown and powerful something clutch at my heart from beyond the solitude. It was my first dim conception that I was an *I*, that I had a soul, and that it had been touched—somehow—from somewhere!

This and similar experiences need no explanation. They show us soul situations which not only point in the direction of changes, but which contain deeply essential things in the form of longing and aspiration for perfection. It is a basic feeling, a romantic one, arising out of the inkling of a new contact with the I. Consciousness becomes stronger. Before this the young person could not separate himself from his feelings, whereas he is now in a position to think about them. He can think about himself. Yet the child is not yet mature enough to stand the very first beginnings of separation, of isolation, which come with thinking about oneself, and which are none of his doing. He cannot yet transform them into self-dependency. This is the beginning of human isolation. A more conscious grasp of the human I. The young person looks for the possible means of coping with life. To a certain extent dolls are played with again, and sometimes even more intensely than before. 'Couldn't I cancel it all out, go back to where I was?'

On the other hand the breaking down of the mother tongue begins. This can only happen because of the emergence of a cognitive force. With the appearance of ego consciousness children begin to become active in their thinking. There is a greater difference between sleeping and waking than there was before. Working in groups, young people receive and create a magical-ritualistic use of language. This functions in ways that do not apply in the family circle. An instinctive resistance against the language used previously now takes precedence. This acquires its force through resisting the function which language had in the children's early years. A sign of this new experience of the ego is that children deliberately create gaps in the previously existing unity between signs and meanings. Throughout the world children of this age invent their own similar dances, symbols, parodies and word puzzles. Most of them arise on the basis of sound, and they parody the meaning.[56] It is a joy to them to break away from their mother tongue, and in many cases it is connected with invisible aggression towards adults or groups of children. Something like conscience awakens with regard to their fellows. All in all it points to a general loosening of everything that arose earlier through the forces of intuition belonging to the kind of consciousness that worked in unison with the environment.

The children's independence is awakening in a limited area without the children themselves being aware of it. In consequence of the loss of the old oneness there appears a more and more subjective experiencing of their world of feeling. The first thing the ego consciousness, which is now appearing in thinking, does, is to bring chaos to the child's former way of feeling. It becomes clear to the child that this belongs only to him and not to the world. Because of this the child cannot attach himself again to the kind of experience of the world which he has lost. In other words: the oneness of the attentiveness of childhood, which had a thoughtlike-feeling character and was of the nature of will and was receptive, has split into its components and, in separation, these are becoming stronger.

The child's intentionally-directed attentiveness and the kind of feeling that repels influences coming from outside have become stronger. The growing youngster rejects any direct influence.

It does not matter what the quality is or the content of the force working to influence him. The child just wants to assert his very own strength. He has this obscure conviction, and this prevents adults from endeavouring to change anything. This is not a reference to the negative stream of feeling raging in the entertainment industry, which addresses not only the conscious personality. This will certainly have an effect on young people in many instances. But young people will more easily be able to resist this if they are given patience and understanding.

The previous intimate association of word signs and meaning is abolished, i.e. children begin to listen to the words and their sound elements. They look for the inner force of language and the form element in it which will support their feeling, and they also seek tangible meaning. Not a conventional meaning, but a more truthful one, one that is basically human; one that is not shallow but more profound than the one they have known up till then. Their capacity to think is released from a fixed connection with language. Their attention is now drawn to poetry, because the sphere of feeling in language can be separated out from the unity of thinking, feeling and will. After a chaotic period of transition a child can now acquire an inner relation to language and its usage. Children leave the picture world of fairytales behind them and start drawing on the world of concepts arising from the consequences and images of events, which means they turn to the realm of thinking. They liberate themselves from the kind of world experience they previously lived in, from the priority of the life of perception. A new possibility opens up for their inner life; a world which is not perceptible at all or no longer solely perceptible. The ability to engage in thinking, in abstraction, arises. This is the period for discussion and argument. Children have a need for dialogues with adults who can help to liberate them from this chaotic experience of language.

What is required of adults is a cultured use of language that comes from the depths of their soul: an absolutely sincere way of speaking. Attentive listening to words and the possibilities of dialogue provide the chance of satisfying, temporarily, in the most dignified way, the longing for unity which cannot be achieved on our earth. This longing arises through having to do without the lost unity, and this is where the unfolding of a human being's individual core takes place—this longing is the activating force for everything in life. We certainly grow through passing through crises, but each person in their own way. People may find quite different solutions to their problems than we might ever have imagined.

When they first went to school, and the children were given religious stories in fairytale form, they transferred their inner devotion to the wonders of the physical world (nature) and also to the divine world, which adults can no longer experience. They did not ask 'Is that true?' Children ask this question when the attitude in the environment and the content of conversations provokes it. That is, when they are torn out of the environment of their natural consciousness. They then express their 'disbelief' using the adults' vocabulary. Before their ninth year children have no independent thoughts on this theme. This would be quite alien to their childlike consciousness, but not to that of star children.

If children have been taught to pray before their ninth year or have made up prayers of their own, something of this spontaneous religiousness can be salvaged for later. Religious feelings left over from their early years live on as memories. They have a yearning for this, but they can no longer awaken in themselves the feelings they once had of reverent trust. Worries, even prickings of conscience overcome them, because the roots of their moral existence are suddenly laid in their own hands. Is there an adult who does not remember the feeling of insecurity connected with this? On the basis of this uncertainty the outside world is criticized more and more, accompanied by an unpleasant feeling experience. To silence this, criticism is stepped up even more, followed by a bad mood of even greater proportions.

Faith is enveloped in darkness. A spark of it leads to enthusiasm for various moral ideas. These often contradict one another and, one after the other, are given short-lived actuality. The ideas predominate for an even shorter time the greater the independence with which the young person masters them. Fundamentally, what young people are looking for is to get their basic faith to spring to life with sufficient intensity that the roots of their moral being can connect up with it.

Adults should not make any endeavour to re-enliven the religious feelings brought from childhood, with the intention of giving the child back its lost treasure. With restraint and tact they can help the child not to reject altogether what it experienced before, and which is being presented to him in a new form. Spontaneous religiousness has been lost, but will ripen latently beneath the surface if it is not disturbed. It is necessary that it withdraws beneath the surface if it is to appear again as the kind of thing that can connect up with the so-called ultimate questions, instead of escaping into compromises, externalities and conformism.

In this period of adolescence it is a good thing to bring children in touch, by way of reading matter, conversation or lessons, with the destinies of individuals who have shown great courage in overcoming the greatest difficulties, as for example the great discoverers and their sea voyages.

Towards the end of their twelfth year children are especially open to parables from the Gospels. Adults should try as far as possible not to tell these directly. For example they can introduce them as being told by somebody else. 'When my teacher was twelve years old he was told this by a wise man.' This allows for space between the parable and the religious feeling.

At this age religious feeling is asleep in the thinking-will. This is the direction in which the individually unfolding religious element will emerge. As soon as the child notices that he is capable of setting his thinking in motion through a kind of thinking-will, then this will re-appear in the awakening newly-arising power of thinking in which the I incarnates.

Through experiencing this a person actually becomes aware that he has the possibility of raising himself to a level of his very own human dignity. The independence, the ability to handle thinking and will, and confidence, fill him once more with admiration and gratitude, with real, intense joy and peace. The activated will in a certain sense holds itself apart from the slumbering religious feeling within him, because at this time, when the young person is acquiring practice in the ability to be abstract, it is functioning in an element that is solely of a thought nature. It is helpful to cultivate, alongside this, a concrete observation of nature, language, and a relationship to the word, and an ongoing, professional learning of an art (the playing of a musical instrument, painting, or something of that kind). By means of this type of activity the young person opens up a way of objectifying his feelings with the help of his newly-awakened faculty in the realm of thought. The subjective quality of feeling is liberated. Through thus becoming engaged, thinking finds the door to the lost unity, and by doing so coaxes feeling into the light of day. As paradoxical as this remark may seem—thinking bears anew the force of receptive feeling. This is to be understood in the following way: This receptive feeling finds a neutral resting-point in abstract, observer thinking, thus liberating feeling from the pressure of the intellect. Meaning that it is not forced to participate as a factor in the activity of intentional, controlled thinking attentiveness. As a feeling of conviction it gently accompanies thinking: and a part of the feeling can unite with the will and with the thinking as a force of knowing. If the young person has developed through artistic education a sense of beauty, he is then in a position to listen to and to take in with his feeling things he did not know before. The feeling is not dependent on old structures of habit. It is open and expectant in a new way.

With the distressing approach of ego consciousness, thinking, feeling and will have, in unison, left the age of childhood. During the before-mentioned crises in the course of which feeling had to suffer the most, the ego has brought strength to the self-awareness in thinking. A non-sentimental compassion has developed at the same time. The self-awareness (present in thinking) has liberated thinking from being embedded in feeling, and lent it wings. When a young person's thinking begins developing and becomes free of subjective feeling the young person can consciously ask questions regarding his moral development. Abstract thinking shows him the intellectual power of human nature. And now for the first time it becomes possible for him to approach consciously the source of intuitive power and to look there for the oneness of thought power and morality. The question becomes all the more important for the young person the fewer 'ultimate' answers he gets. He will be interested in the events in the life of Jesus Christ if, prior to this he has, during his chaotic period, become acquainted with Parsifal and other human beings with heroic 'faith'. This search can release him in this area from fear of going astray and from dilettantism. If in his endeavours he has the necessary freedom in his thinking, he will clearly realize that he cannot reckon on rapid results.

No-one can be taught to have religious feeling, for it lives in a person. It is shaky and not lasting if it arises solely spontaneously or lacks thinking and will—i.e. science and art. If the inherent religious feeling, which is to be regarded as we saw as part of the whole of the young person's evolution, disappears or arises again free and sound, this does not depend ultimately on people of the child's own generation but on those who came into the world earlier than he did.

It is getting increasingly more difficult to say anything about children or young people that is generally valid, because their individual nature is appearing more and more strongly at an earlier and earlier age. This applies to an even greater extent to star children. What can help those responsible for the child in this respect is the conviction that every child—just like every human being—is creative, and that thanks to this creative force all children will make the transition from childhood to adolescence. The cultivation of the creative element in children consists largely in adults not interfering in their individual—and in this respect inscrutable—development; this should lead nowadays to creativity in everyone.

APPENDIX II
Meditations

Meditation

Everyone makes use of deductive thinking, which moves from concept to concept, from one word to the next, and in addition—though far less often—intuitive thinking, that usually proceeds like lightning, in pictures, wordlessly, and only becomes conscious in its results. This kind of thinking enables us to understand concepts and to create new ones. We use the first kind of thinking for exchanging information. We do, however, have the kind of experiences which cannot be communicated by means of informative speech: for example all experience of an artistic kind which originates in aesthetic feeling and appeals to this. Informative speaking also has its origin in what is usually a superconscious, wordless *something* which is above language. It has to be there so that we can find the right words and grammatical forms (that, too, is usually an unconscious process), after we have decided, should the occasion arise, in which language the communication shall be given. The wordless *thing*, the sense or meaning, is translated and can be translated, as it arises beyond languages and is understood as such: The one who thinks the thing has to 'ignore' the words, become free of them, if he is to understand the meaning of the sentence. Experiences which cannot be communicated either in an informative or an artistic way are called spiritual experiences. They usually have to do with fundamental questions about the nature of the world, man, reality, the spirit and the soul; for instance with the sphere that words and concepts come from and which obviously cannot themselves be described in words or concepts. Experiences of this kind can be communicated in texts for meditation or in symbolic images. This kind of text is not informative, not graspable by reason, and usually also paradoxical; the images indicate a meaning which can neither be put into words nor depict sense reality. Meditative texts can be found in the Bible, in the words of Buddha and the Bodhidarmas, and in texts by numerous mystics and also Rudolf Steiner.

Meditating on texts

We recognize a meditative text through the fact that if we understand it solely as information it leaves the infallible feeling behind that we have not understood its whole meaning. When we encounter this kind of text we should first of all try to approach it with concentrated thinking. This activity can be called 'contemplation'. The aim is to apply all the possibilities thinking offers in order to determine as far as we can the various words and the structure of the sentence, and then we give it up when we have discovered that thinking is incapable of it. Thinking gets 'tired', so that it does not start disturbing the meditation.

Meditating means concentrating on the meaning of the sentence, i.e. on the formal, informative kind of meaning, which is what one could translate without understanding the real, deeper meaning of the sentence. So we can, for example, try out an exercise with the sentence: 'Words come from the wordless element.' The translatable sentence, which can be understood in a formal sense, contains the word 'wordless' that to begin with is not an experience, which is why it seems puzzling that something can 'come' from it. Concentrating on the formal (informative, translatable) sense of the text is made more difficult through the fact that it appears in several words even though we can only concentrate on *one* sign. We can either take the whole sentence as a unity or reduce it to one single word which then represents the whole sentence. The best thing to do is to choose a word from the sentence (but not an article) and one after the other put the meaning of the other words into this simple word. For example we choose the little word 'from' and let 'from' absorb 'come': 'Words from the wordless element.' Then we drop 'words' and put its meaning into 'from': 'From the wordless element.' We finally condense 'the wordless element' into 'from' as well. And we now concentrate on this final word which now means the whole of the text. This last sign usually disappears too, but the sense of it remains in our concentrated attentiveness—a signless 'thing'. If our concentration is sufficiently intense, an experience can occur intuitively like a flash of lightning, of the hidden sense of the sentence: We discover the wordless reality. If we repeat the same meditation we arrive every time at other more profound intuitions, which supplement one another and take other ones further, without our ever having arrived at a final 'complete' insight, for we are changed by our experiences and, to the person who is being changed, the text constantly says new things which had previously remained hidden. Wordless, conceptfree, *pure* thinking can become transformed into perceptive feeling and this again into receptive will.

When meditating, essentially the same discoveries are made as with the concentration exercise. This prepares us, when meditating, to be able to concentrate in the necessary way on signless meaning. The experiences we have are an identifying with the theme and the I am experience.

Meditating on symbolic images

Symbolic images are signs presenting a meaning which cannot be communicated in any other way. They can either be static or depict a process. An example of this kind of image is a pond surrounded by trees; a wild duck is sitting on the bank who then walks into the water and swims across the pond. Reaching the other side it climbs on to the bank, turns to face the water and, whilst standing on one leg, and putting its beak and its head under its feathers, it lowers itself into a 'meditative' position. The meditation begins with calling up the picture of the opening scene: The pond, the bank and the wild duck. As with the concentration exercise, this can be done by means of the inner gesture, the silent question: 'What do you look like?' Doing it this way the picture arises as a memory, even if we have never seen one like it. Then we make way for the action: we watch the duck swimming, and even see the waves it is producing in the water. When the action is finished we first of all hold the picture that has arisen (of the duck on the bank after crossing the water); then, however, we endeavour to grasp the whole action as a unity in our feeling. Every image is noteworthy. If the meditation is successful we experience an understanding in feeling. This is actually not translatable into words, or rather we can formulate a lot of 'interpretations'. It is best we avoid such formulations and remain in the feeling experience. As with the concentration exercise the appearance of cognitive feeling depends on the intensity of the attentiveness.

When this exercise has been repeated successfully several times you can practise it in a more difficult form, namely that the duck's swimming leaves the water undisturbed — no waves arise.

We can find symbolic images in any fairytale. These are

pictures presented in text form in a similar way to the Lord's parables in the New Testatament, e.g. the picture of the sower (Mark 4).

Meditating on perceptions

Natural objects, in common with meditative texts and symbolic images, have a meaning which cannot be communicated informatively. For natural phenomena are signs for immense ideas which are far more powerful than any meanings created by human beings — including those in the realm of art. However, these ideas are rayed out by the phenomena. In meditating on perceptions we endeavour to approach the irradiating of these ideas. Any of our senses can be used for this; the easiest way is to start with sight. Except when taking in works of art, we are familiar in our everyday life with a feeling kind of seeing, namely in eye contact and looking at a human face. In the case of eye contact the gaze of both partners is receptive; it is the same with looking at a face, if we look at it as a totality, in a way that is not directed at details but at the total impression of the face, so that we do not even need to perceive details. We shall recognize that face again and can visualize it without knowing for example how the nose is formed. Let us try to look at a simple natural object (a pebble, a leaf) with this kind of looking.

A preparatory exercise consists of looking at the object as a whole in a concentrated way for about half a minute, avoiding as far as possible applying any descriptions 'in words', i.e. any kind of conceptual cataloguing of details, and then, with closed eyes or looking the other way, we visualize what we have seen. This serves to separate the otherwise lightning oscillations of our attention between perceiving (abandon) and conceptual realization of what we have seen. In visualizing we are at any rate 'in ourselves' and have not abandoned ourselves to the object.

The more often we repeat this preparatory exercise, even if we shorten the time of looking, the more surely we shall succeed with the subsequent meditation. This is prepared by applying the sort of looking which is 'scientific' and analytical, directed at details and working with concepts, and you do this for about half a minute, accompanying it by a feeling that something—attentiveness—is streaming from you to the object. This is followed by closing our eyes for a second—blinking—after which we look at the object again, this time with a receptive, inviting kind of eye contact, as though we were saying: 'Come along', 'Show me what you are,' 'Talk to me'. And this is accompanied by the feeling that something is now streaming from the object to us. This phase is the actual meditation of a perception, and it is held as long as we are experiencing something different compared to how we felt whilst we were looking analytically. If there is no difference, we go on doing the preparatory exercise. The 'difference' is experienced in feeling. If we were to put it into words—which are never quite exact—we would say: The object grows larger, comes closer, gets warmer, softer, brighter; its being grows stronger, it breathes and pulsates, it is alive and in a state of becoming. If we intensify this exercice we can experience how our attentiveness is shaped by the object, which is an I experience. By comparing our meditation on different objects our perceptive feeling takes hold of things in greater and greater detail until it is raised to a feeling for quality (similar to the way it happens in the aesthetic realm with the specific feelings regarding music, painting, sculpture, etc.).

This kind of meditating has the characteristic that when

we concentrate fairly strongly it succeeds quite easily the first time. When repeating it we have expectations due to the first easy successes, and these are obviously a hindrance.

Openmindedness

We human beings are constantly being confronted with things that are new and unknown, with new situations, problems and phenomena, and where the new children are concerned this can be experienced more and more acutely. Obviously we endeavour to get on top of these new phenomena by falling back on past experience, and this can happen in two ways. We can compare the new with the old, and judge and solve new situations by drawing on previous experience. In past, pre-Christian times this was a justified procedure: laws and mythological pictures, experienced deeply in the feelings, served as models for finding our bearings in life. In the age of freedom in which we now live, past experiences should not be used directly as models of conduct but be transformed into the corresponding faculties: just as an artist acquires the ability, through his pictures, to paint new pictures, and does not merely repeat those he has painted before. We all drag a great many opinions, preconceptions and prejudices along with us which, without our being conscious of it, arose largely through our education. It certainly makes sense to look at these things from time to time. Apart from the prejudices which can be perceived and overcome comparatively easily we have habits of thought, of feeling and of will which are more difficult to be aware of because they determine the whole structure of our consciousness. This sort of bias arises for instance by way of the mother tongue in our thinking, for the very first formative influence on our thinking is formed by the word concepts and grammar inherent in it. Learning a foreign language helps to a large extent to overcome the restrictedness and to experience the element that is above language and concepts, where concepts arise and are understood. In the concentration exercise we meet the object as a wordless *thing* in the centre of our attentiveness; although it is still an abstraction, it is not connected with a sign. In the course of meditating, informative, formal understanding of a sentence or a picture dissolves in order to move towards a new understanding: in the transition the consciousness is free of concepts without losing its concentration. This phenomenon makes it clear to us that concept-free concentration can only arise in concentrated attentiveness.

This level of openmindedness is the prerequisite for any kind of creative activity including the realm of pedagogy. A person's being, the soul/spiritual structure of the child at that moment, can only be grasped intuitively, which means in concept-free attentiveness, and where this is concerned clinging in any way to theories, concepts and past experience is hampering. Help can come from the past only if our various experiences are transformed into capacities. It is like this with everything we have learnt. We have to learn a great deal to be able to forget it. But what our consciousness acquires through learning and forgetting is the ability to create, ourselves, structures similar to the structures of the things we have learnt.

Afterword

Since this book was published in Germany much has been written about it in various periodicals, either to acknowledge it or to criticize it. A considerable part of the criticism was below the level of possible discussion, being founded on misunderstandings due to superficial reading, and to emotions of a subjective nature. Some of it sprang from good will, and I would like to reply to the authors of those contributions.

I do not think there is any doubt about the phenomenon, namely that the number of 'deviating' children (deviating from what?) is growing rapidly; but there may be differences in finding the reasons. We can exclude the view that the brains of these children are in some way defective. First of all no research has proved able to support this statement, and even if deviations could be found in the chemistry of the brain these could well be consequences and not causes. Similarly we can exclude heredity as being the cause — there is no evidence or indication of this. So there remain two possible explanations: that the phenomenon is caused by a) altered circumstances, e.g. parents have neither time nor energy to bring up their children, who thus get more and more TV, computer games and other 'bad' influences. Or b) there is a steep change in the development of humanity as a whole, as was the case in the thirteenth century, in the Renaissance, and in the romantic period.

In the past decade mainstream child psychology has discovered, besides heredity and the effect of the environment, a third factor of life, possibly the main one, namely individuality. The effects of the environment are taken up very selectively, so its influence seems to diminish as the children become more and more individual. The 'response' to this influence is individual again, the child possibly even developing a resistance to it (resilience). Identical twins (conjoined twins, children growing up in the same environment) show enormous differences in their individuality. There is no significant difference in the children who come from families raising them consciously or from families that do not care much about them. In a similar way it is evident that the advent of this new kind of child is happening all over the globe, on all continents and among all nations.

The main characteristic of this new generation—and here I do not restrict myself to star children but am endeavouring to include all 'difficult' children—is to be open, more open than the adult world used to experience children. Openness means not being separated from the spiritual world, from the world of meaning, from being conscious of the human environment, from the source of intuitions—by preserving the cognitive feeling through which every small child gets the meaning of the first, say, 1,000 words and of the grammatical forms in acquiring speech. It means also that the child does not experience the world in a dualistic manner as adults do, with the feeling that 'I am here and the world is there'. These children experience the world like adults experience a theatre performance, identifying with the plot—therefore being moved, sometimes to tears. It means that children preserve the faculties and attitudes of the small child longer, sometimes for the whole of life. But at the same time this means that these children will have difficulties adapting to the form of society's thinking, feeling and will, and will have difficulties in school. They will be much less intellectual than people want them to be, they will have problems in most lessons that require intellectuality, memorizing, intellectually-formed concepts, focusing on themes they find uninteresting at the time, and sitting for long hours without much contact with things that are easily experienced through feelings, such as nature and art. Maintaining the 'terrible' habit of a two-year-old to be in constant movement, they will be judged at school or even at kindergarten level as 'hyperactive'. Most of them have a very strong self-awareness from the beginning (immediately after birth) as the way they look at you shows. Feeling equal to adults in respect of human relationships they do not tolerate orders 'from above'. In fact, seeing, as they do, through any disguise put up by adults they have not often any reason to take them as authorities.

In their contact with adults the negative sides of openness will be uppermost, and the positive sides — talents for the arts, social faculties, the will to help — usually go unnoticed. As these children do not develop the 'normal' kind of egotism built on autoperception, on the feeling for the body, they construct, after a series of frustrations, a secondary form of egotism as a defense, and this makes the situation still more difficult — in fact a vicious circle of emotional turmoil.

Children — and even adults — are becoming more and more 'spiritual', which means almost the opposite of being clever, intellectually involved, like our ancestors were in earlier times, but they were then without self-awareness. This development towards a more spiritual humanity has been foretold in the works of R. Steiner, J. Gebser and Ortega y Gasset. There are various reasons why many adults resist acknowledging this situation. The most important causes are the following:

a) Any deviation from what we are used to experiencing in children is easily taken as pathological.

b) To understand the soul/spiritual make-up of the new generation requires a profound change in our world view as well as new faculties for the acquisition of individual understanding—classification according to type does not work in the majority of cases.*

c) Humanly—all too humanly—we feel that anything that is 'different from me' has to be corrected or repaired.

The danger is that by not changing firstly our views and then our faculties we are destroying the possibility of the change these children could bring about in humanity, the change to a more human way of life in which the ruling factor would cease to be egotism.

Georg Kühlewind
January 2004

---

*For decades now autistic people have been considered retarded, lacking in intelligence, schizophrenic, etc., because their defensive gestures are mistaken for primary symptoms. We know nowadays that they can be highly intelligent, but can express themselves mostly only by FC (facilitated communication). Their chief characteristic is that they are very open, not separated from other people, and their defensive reserve is to compensate for this inner make-up.

Notes

1. See Kühlewind *Der sprechende Mensch*, Klostermann, Frankfurt/Main 1991, chapter III.2; and *Das Licht des Wortes*, Stuttgart 1984, chapter II.
2. Lev Vygotsky *Thought and Language*, The MIT Press 1999, chapter 2.
3. Kühlewind *Aufmerksamkeit und Hingabe*, Stuttgart 1998, chapters 6, 7 and 8; and *Der sanfte Wille*, Stuttgart 2000, chapter II.
4. In pre-birth existence, being is at the same time a speaking, an utterance of the soul's own being. See R. Steiner *Geisteswissenschaftliche Menschenkunde*, (Complete Edition 107), Dornach 1988, lecture of 26 October 1908.
5. The Logos Foundation (1995 New Jersey, USA; 1996 Hungary) was founded for (in the broadest sense) neglected children. Its activity covers courses for parents and teachers, which are primarily about small children and how to treat them; in the USA there is also training for and maintenance of nursery schools.
6. *Aufmerksamkeit und Hingabe*, op. cit., chapters 3 and 4.
7. There are descriptions of concentration and meditation exercises both in Appendix II of the present book and in Kühlewind *From Normal to Healthy. Paths to the Liberation of Consciousness*, Lindisfarne Press, Great Barrington 1988, chapters 5.3 and 5.4; and Kühlewind *Die Belehrung der Sinne*, Stuttgart 1990, chapter 8; and *Aufmerksamkeit und Hingabe*, op. cit., chapter 23; and *Der Sanfte Wille*, op. cit., chapter IV.
8. Conditioned reflexes (Pavlov) or stimulus response mechanisms do not signify understanding.
9. The exclamation 'We look beautiful!' can have at least two different meanings. Someone who can read is not induced to do so by invisible lines of force (e.g. magnetic forces) but by connections invisible to the senses (and which cannot be

made visible) existing between the letters, the words and so on.

10. Standing upright, walking, etc. are initially gestures of expression. When the child performs them it is not doing so for a purpose but simply demonstrates its human nature. By walking to its mother it is making a statement.

11. See chapters 9 and 12 in the present book; and *Das Licht des Wortes*, op. cit., chapter II; and *Der sprechende Mensch*, op. cit., chapter III.2.

12. As language is not inherited, thinking in a language can also not be inherited.

13. Kühlewind *Meditationen über Zen-Buddhismus, Thomas von Aquin und Anthroposophie*, Stuttgart 1999, chapter 2.

14. Kühlewind *Der Gral oder was die Liebe vermag*, edition tertium, Ostfildern 1997, chapter 3; and Kühlewind *Die Esoterik des Erkennens und Handelns*, Stuttgart 1995, chapter VI.

15. *Der Sanfte Wille*, op. cit., chapter IV.

16. R. Steiner *At Home in the Universe* (Complete Edition 231) Anthroposophic Press, Hudson 2000, lecture of 14 November 1923: 'The way we speak and express ourselves in fleeting words, if you imagine this as a means of self-expression, as a revelation of our very being, then you have a picture of the way human beings, with their different natures, meet and manifest themselves between death and a new birth. Word encounters word, articulated word meets articulated word, inwardly enlivened word encounters inwardly enlivened word. And the human beings themselves are these words, and their sounding together is the sounding together of the essence of the being of the articulated word. Impermeability does not exist there: human beings really live one with another, and the word which is one person's being merges with the word which is another person's being. This is where those karmic connections are formed, the effects of which stay with us in our following earth life, and which come to expression when people meet, in the way they relate to one another and feel a kind of sympathy and antipathy for one another. This kind of feeling

is an echo of the way human beings encountered one another in the land of the spirit in the middle of the time between death and a new birth. The way we spoke to one another, there, was that the speaking was we ourselves, and all that we now have of this on earth is a shadowy copy in our feelings.' (See also the lecture referred to in Note 4.)

17. *Der sanfte Wille*, op. cit., chapters 'Wege zur Erfahrung der Gegenwärtigkeit' and 'Der kosmische Hintergrund des sanften Willens'.

18. That something exists independently of human beings can only be determined by a being that is non-human. This hypothesis also claims that existence accords with what human beings know of it and that this matter of existence remains the same even if human knowledge changes.

19. *Der Gral oder was die Liebe vermag*, op. cit., chapter 1.

20. Similar processes of transformation in different sense realms were described by R. Steiner in *The Riddle of Humanity* (Complete Edition 170) Rudolf Steiner Press, London 1990, lecture of 2 September 1916.

21. R. Steiner *The Riddle of Man* (Complete Edition 20), Mercury Press, Spring Valley 1990; and *Der sanfte Wille*, op. cit., second appendix.

22. Research has shown that some languages use the same word to describe taste and smell; hearing, the sense of words and the sense of thought do not become separate in children until quite late on; the word 'to feel' can cover very large sense areas, all according to which language is used.

23. A well-known example of this is the palette of colours: in numerous languages it is differently arranged than, for example, in the German language. See *Der sprechende Mensch*, op. cit., p.53.

24. This process is described in greater detail in chapters 11 and 12.

25. Pre-Socratic philosophers must surely have meant something quite different by the words 'fire', 'water', 'air' and 'earth' than we usually do.

26. The first syllable uttered by a baby (ma, ba, da etc.) signifies the whole world, the first structuring.

27. Described further in *Aufmerksamkeit und Hingabe*, op. cit., chapters 7, 13 and 18; also *Der sanfte Wille*, op. cit., exercises 19 to 21.

28. *Aufmerksamkeit und Hingabe*, op. cit., chapters 19 and 25.

29. Ibid., chapters 13 and 18.

30. With regard to the Fall, which is repeated in every child, there are two comments to be made. The first is connected with two passages in Genesis. In 2,25 we read: 'And they were both naked, the man and his wife, and were not ashamed.' And in 3,7–11 we see: 'And [due to the Fall] the eyes of them both were opened, and they knew that they were naked; and they sewed fig leaves together, and made themselves aprons... And the Lord God called unto Adam, and said unto him, Where art thou? And he said: I heard thy voice in the garden, and I was afraid, because I was naked, and I hid myself. And he said: Who told thee that thou wast naked? Hast thou eaten of the tree...?' Before the Fall, the human being's *body* was naked, not *himself*. After the Fall he feels himself as body, and *he* now becomes naked. The call: Adam, where art thou? Indicates a sudden falling away from the state of oneness. The second comment is this: Those who speak of duality and experience it must have an element at work in them which is not subject to the duality, otherwise they would not be able to experience it. This element has so little self-awareness that its presence is usually not noticed at all. Something similar occurs when, for instance, we compare two languages. We do not notice that, to do this, we need to apply a kind of thinking which is both independent of language and above it. To notice this would be the first step to a realization of the true self. (See Note 29.)

31. See Kühlewind in the periodical *Das Goetheanum*, Nos. 19–22, 2001.

32. See *Der sanfte Wille*, op. cit., chapter III.

33. R. Steiner *Der Goetheanismus, ein Umwandlungsimpuls und Auferstehungsgedanke* (Complete Edition 188), Dornach 1982,

lecture of 10 January 1919; also R. Steiner *The Case for Anthroposophy* (extracts from *Von Seelenrätseln* Complete Edition 21), Rudolf Steiner Press, London 1970, chapters I and IV/3.

34. R. Steiner *The World of the Senses and the World of the Spirit* (Complete Edition 134), Steiner Book Centre, Vancouver 1979, lecture of 28 December 1911.

35. A similar experience can occur if there is a momentary flashing up of receptive attentiveness when, coming from concentrating in one's thinking and visualizing, one has one's first glimpse of the sense world—it then seems to blossom anew. This also happens if one realizes receptive attentiveness in sense perception. (See *Die Belehrung der Sinne*, op. cit., chapter 8.3.) In both cases thinking has to be silent.

36. *Der sanfte Wille*, op. cit., chapter III.

37. See Note 33.

38. *Aufmerksamkeit und Hingabe*, op. cit., chapters 13 and 18.

39. *Der sanfte Wille*, op. cit., exercises 9 and 17; interim remark p.80.

40. *Das Licht des Wortes*, op. cit., chapter II.

40a. See Note 28.

41. *Der sanfte Wille*, op. cit., exercise 7.

42. Ibid., exercise 9.

43. *Aufmerksamkeit und Hingabe*, op. cit., chapter 4.

44. *Der sanfte Wille*, op. cit., exercise 8.

45. Ibid., exercise, chapter IV; and *Aufmerksamkeit und Hingabe*, op. cit., chapter 24.

46. *Die Belehrung der Sinne*, op. cit., chapter 8. Relevant texts by R. Steiner are in the Appendix.

47. Regarding the inner attitude of adults to children I recommend the books by Henning Köhler, especially *Schwierige Kinder gibt es nicht*, Stuttgart 2001, and *Was haben wir nur falsch gemacht?*, Stuttgart 2000.

48. For exercises in overcoming prejudice see Appendix II in the present book; also *From Normal to Healthy*, op. cit., chapter 5.5, exercise 5; also *Der sanfte Wille*, exercise 24.

49. *Die Belehrung der Sinne,* op. cit., chapter 1.
50. *Aufmerksamkeit und Hingabe,* op. cit., chapters 5–8.
51. Thomas Aquinas gives a brilliant description of the difference between intuitive and rational thinking. See *Meditationen über Zen-Buddhismus, Thomas von Aquin und Anthroposophie,* op. cit., chapter 4, p.69.
52. For meditating on images see Appendix II in the present book, and also *Der sanfte Wille,* op. cit., chapter IV.
53. J. Lusseyran *And There Was Light,* Heinemann, London 1964.
54. Included in Ineke Verschuren (ed.) *Die Reise zur Sonne. Geschichten zu Ostern, Pfingsten und Johanni,* Stuttgart, 2nd edition 1996. Also in L. Schlesselmann *Die christlichen Jahresfeste und ihre Bräuche,* new edition, Stuttgart 2001.
55. B. Walter *Theme and Variations,* Hamish Hamilton, London 1947.
56. See H. Müller-Wiedemann *Mitte der Kindheit,* 4th edition, Stuttgart 1994.